Transforming Teaching

Transforming Teaching shares the successes and the problems that were solved by a diverse group of educators during the global pandemic. The shared stories from around the globe will help and inspire any teacher to develop skills to support blended learning in whatever teaching situation they find themselves.

Including lessons to be learned from Kindergarten to University, this book introduces new ways of working and pedagogical approaches appropriate for developing global skills. It importantly focuses on teacher narratives to aid personal reflection and encourages readers to take responsibility for their own professional development. Each chapter prompts teachers to reflect and build on new skills developed through distance and blended learning, use of technology and new ways of relating to students.

Responding to an educational need at a time of crisis, this book is essential reading to all who are interested in the future potential of education and those who want to shape future emerging practice.

Lucy Cooker is the Director of Taught Courses in the School of Education at the University of Nottingham.

Tony Cotton is a writer and educational consultant.

Helen Toft is an assistant professor on the PGCEi course at the University of Nottingham.

'*Transforming Teaching: Lessons Learned from Teaching Under Lockdown* is both an important contribution to recent educational discussion and a book which reaches deep into the future. The book draws on voices from around the world, to take a critical position with respect to the formation of future educational possibilities. I fully recommend *Transforming Teaching: Lessons Learned from Teaching Under Lockdown* to all who are interested in the future potential of education'.

Ole Skovsmose, *Aalborg University, Denmark and Universidade Estadual Paulista, Sao Paulo, Brazil*

'This book is a celebration of what makes teaching such a messy, complex, challenging and yet fulfilling profession. Lucy, Tony and Helen have sensitively curated the voices of educators at a time of global change. These voices hold a mirror to us as educators and ask us to reflect critically on our own practices and their impact on children. They offer ways forward to reimagine education if we choose. An essential read'.

Dr Pinky Jain, *Principal Lecturer in Primary Education and School International Lead, Worcester University, UK*

'Through reflective conversations with educators across the world, this book maps a critical cartography of our time in Covid-19. It provides a hopeful space to re-imagine our values and ethics within these times and beyond. I would recommend any person in Education who wants to shape future emerging practice to engage with these global narratives'.

Lisa Stephenson, *Course Leader MA Drama & Creative Writing in Education and Director/Founder of Story Makers Company*

'This book is an invitation for educators to immerse themselves into the authors' personal stories, experiences and reflections and start a professional dialogue around the key question: "What really matters in education in a post-pandemic world."

As the educational world changed all around us the three main authors began to collect and share professional and personal insights not only of their experiences but also those of global educators. They offer us the opportunity to annotate as we read, guiding us to pause and reflect upon our own experiences in the hope that we take this opportunity to consider our own learning and how this can shape the future of a more global, compassionate education for all.

The stories are a truly enjoyable read and give a sense of realism and optimism. For me, the reflective questions invited me to dig deep, stimulating new perspectives and possibilities in the International work I do for the Curriculum Foundation and as a school improvement director for a Multi-academy trust'.

Narinder Gill, *Strategic Director for the Curriculum Foundation*

'The Covid 19 pandemic precipitated a significant paradigm shift for teachers, students and schools (and others too, of course). So many steep learning curves, so many personal journeys, so many problems and solutions and shifts in our thinking. We'll be talking about them for years. Tony, Helen and Lucy had the foresight to try and capture these stories as they were happening and facilitate that dialogue. Everyone has been so immersed in their own circumstances that it is easy to get lost in them. In this book, the authors have set out to offer us an important range of circumstances and perspectives that allow us to take a wider look at how this has played out for different people in different places. It allows us to put our own experiences into perspective and in doing so brings more weight to key questions about what educationalists can take and learn from this rare and seismic event that is a great opportunity to re-examine what education's priorities might be. We must not miss the opportunity to do this and we mustn't do it in isolation, imagining that our perspective alone is enough. The personal stories are so authentic and honest, which allows us to empathise with the teachers, their students and their communities and wrestle with their problems and solutions ourselves. The authors then help us put the pieces together and set about those key questions. I most appreciated the way the book very deliberately sets out to challenge us to reflect on our own views, experiences and priorities, following each of the stories and allowing us both the mental and physical space to do so. As such this brings a valuable personal experience to reading the book as well. This is a really important piece of work at a really important time and I thoroughly enjoyed it. Very grateful to the authors and the teachers for writing it for us'.

Jim Noble, *The International School of Tououse, Teacher, Author and Consultant*

'This is a very timely book, appearing as it does when educators across the globe are coming to terms with the jolt that has been felt in their world of learning and teaching. The authors offer a worldwide perspective on the effect of the pandemic upon them personally and professionally and on the way those they help to learn will experience a different form of relationship with learning in the future.

Each chapter provides a stimulus for consideration: of aims, curriculum, pedagogy, personal organisation or future anticipated changes in these. The prompts are followed with prompts for reflection by the reader with the invitation to do things differently in the future.

The analysis of the response to the pandemic in nations around the world is intriguing and the book takes us from the concern about what may have been lost to the prospect of opportunity while recognising the traditional inertia of the education culture and community.

This is an illuminating book, a fascinating read and food for thought for all who want to be part of a global transformation of the power and practice of teaching'.

Professor Mick Waters, *Centre for Developmental and Applied Research with Wolverhampton University, UK*

Transforming Teaching

Global Responses to Teaching Under the Covid-19 Pandemic

Lucy Cooker, Tony Cotton and Helen Toft

LONDON AND NEW YORK

First published 2022
by Routledge
2 Park Square, Milton Park, Abingdon, Oxon OX14 4RN

and by Routledge
605 Third Avenue, New York, NY 10158

Routledge is an imprint of the Taylor & Francis Group, an informa business

© 2022 Lucy Cooker, Tony Cotton and Helen Toft

The right of Lucy Cooker, Tony Cotton and Helen Toft to be identified as authors of this work has been asserted by them in accordance with sections 77 and 78 of the Copyright, Designs and Patents Act 1988.

All rights reserved. No part of this book may be reprinted or reproduced or utilised in any form or by any electronic, mechanical, or other means, now known or hereafter invented, including photocopying and recording, or in any information storage or retrieval system, without permission in writing from the publishers.

Trademark notice: Product or corporate names may be trademarks or registered trademarks, and are used only for identification and explanation without intent to infringe.

British Library Cataloguing-in-Publication Data
A catalogue record for this book is available from the British Library

Library of Congress Cataloging-in-Publication Data
A catalog record has been requested for this book

ISBN: 978-0-367-71384-3 (hbk)
ISBN: 978-0-367-71385-0 (pbk)
ISBN: 978-1-003-15059-6 (ebk)

DOI: 10.4324/9781003150596

Typeset in Bembo
by Deanta Global Publishing Services, Chennai, India

Contents

Preface ix
Acknowledgements xx

PART 1
Setting the scene 1

1 Introduction 3
2 Educational aims and values for the 21st century 13
3 The contributors and the settings in which they work 31

PART 2
Responding to the pandemic 49

4 How the setting changed as a result of the pandemic 51
5 How relationships with colleagues changed 75
6 How relationships with learners changed 89
7 How relationships with parents and the wider community changed 105
8 My best 'home learning' lesson 119
9 What have we learned from teaching under the pandemic? 135

PART 3
Looking to the future   **149**

10   Innovations that will persist   151

11   A global vision for the future   167

12   Entitlements for all learners   179

      Index   185

Preface

> *To teach in a manner that respects and cares for the souls of our students is essential if we are to provide the necessary conditions where learning can most deeply and intimately begin ...*
>
> (hooks, 1994)

For six months in the middle of 2020 most of the world experienced life without the daily routine of students going into school. The taken-for-granted routine had stopped abruptly. Some suggested that education had ceased. This, of course, was not the case. We cannot stop people from learning. Even if all formal teaching had ceased people would have learned. And learned in new ways. But teaching did not cease. Teachers are innovative people and very quickly found ways in which they could engage with the learners they felt responsible for. Currently (February 2021), different countries are in different situations. As I (Tony) revisit this preface, I have just come off an online meeting with a student of mine in China. He told a familiar story. When the pandemic hit, he and his wife and child moved to the country where his wife's family live (he is Czech, his wife is Chinese). Then, returning to the city and lockdown in his apartment for two months he found himself supporting the young learners he would normally be teaching in a classroom with online teaching. He has decided to use video much more with these learners and is using video as a part of the assessment he must undertake for the course he is on, partly as a result of his experience under lockdown.

Tony and Helen's grandchildren in England are just entering their second period of lockdown. Unlike the first period of online teaching and learning, there was immediate access to online learning and other support from teachers for both of them. Their wonderful teachers are now prepared and so are Felix and Tate. Both learners and teachers have become used to new ways of working and learning. It will be fascinating to see how this develops as Felix and Tate grow older.

The education system is a global system. The international response to the Covid-19 pandemic was a shared one. Schools were closed. Teachers were asked to provide learning experiences at home, often with very short time frames. Parents were asked to support their children in accessing learning at home. Social media around the world showed how teachers were sharing the approaches that they had found successful and working together to solve problems. But in Brazil, our co-author Amanda tells us 'telephone connections were supposed to be available in all areas for apps like *YouTube*'. But some students don't even have a notebook, no way to fund their learning, perhaps only one child in a family can be educated. Parents were working during class time; some didn't have the signal from the phone company because the networks don't go that far out. If a neighbour had a signal too many children would ask to use it at once'.

Reflecting back and looking to the future it appears that the nature of learning and teaching is starting to shift. Lessons under the various 'lockdowns' ceased to exist in a fixed time frame. If they had internet access, learning could be accessed by learners at any time in the day. Students could pick up their learning in bite-sized pieces or as an extended activity. What seems new and radical is that in many cases, learners were making these decisions.

We think that this crisis, which has led to teachers rapidly developing new ways of working, as crises often do, could be a transformative moment in global education. We (that is Lucy, Tony and Helen) started our own conversation building on our previous book, *Being a teacher: Teaching and learning in a global context*, and contacted educators from around the world to test out our hunch that transformative practices were happening. This book formalises and fixes these informal conversations. We argue that the nature of teaching and learning will change as schools around the world return; indeed we suggest that teaching will be transformed as a result of learners and teachers' experiences. We would hope that all teachers are able to learn and draw on the lessons of 'teaching under lockdown' as they develop their classroom practice. The authors of the book have experience in schools across the continents. They have experience in learning and teaching in every phase of education, from Early Years (kindergarten in many parts of the world) to university. So, you, the readers, will be learning global lessons.

Our aim is to share and draw on innovative practices from around the world to support all teachers in developing their repertoire of teaching skills. We think this will be particularly important in supporting and developing blended learning in whatever teaching situation you find yourself. We hope that you will be introduced to new ways of working and to pedagogical approaches appropriate for developing global skills. We have certainly all learned and developed our practice as teachers through researching and writing this book. You will read of the many different ways that educators around the world have supported learners in home settings. This includes ways in which the learners can access the tasks and activities and ways in which parents can be supported in becoming the surrogate teachers or teaching assistants. We also hope that we can all begin to address issues of equity in access to education.

Australian educators found themselves in the enviable position of resuming face-to-face learning sooner than many of their international colleagues. Thus, they have been able to reflect on the practices they adopted during remote learning and use the later stages of the 2020 school year to try some of the more successful and innovative approaches within the classroom setting. This book will expand on the range of experiences that Australian educators can draw upon by sharing stories from educators from around the world. We hope they will provide further inspiration, as educators strive to use the global pandemic to transform their practice.

Lucy, Tony and Helen carried out in-depth interviews with a wide range of educators from around the world. These interviews are then used as the basis for the narratives in each of the chapters.

The author team

Lucy, Tony and Helen are the three core authors who have edited the book. We met whilst working on the University of Nottingham's Post Graduate Certificate of Education (International) course (PGCEi) and teaching in Bangkok. This course, which offers an education qualification to teachers working internationally, has become one of the largest courses, in terms of numbers of participants, in the university. The Bangkok cohort is one of 21 cohorts from across the globe. In previous years an intensive four-day face-to-face experience was followed by a year of online study. As with many other courses we are now carrying out all the teaching online.

We drew on our experiences of working with teachers on the PGCEi to write the book *Being a teacher: Teaching and learning in a global context*. This book drew on the stories of educators working in international contexts to explore what made effective learning and teaching in the global context.

Two Australian authors, Jess Greenbaum and Michael Minas, were part of the team of educators who shared their experiences. Michael has worked in education for 20 years. He began working part-time at a local primary school as an integration aide while he completed his study to become a teacher. He worked for 17 years as a classroom teacher, primarily in the western suburbs of Melbourne and also did a brief stint as a supply teacher in London. Michael is now the director of Love Maths, an education consulting company that specialises in numeracy. His areas of interest include problem solving and student engagement. In 2018, Michael's ability to shape learning beyond the classroom was recognised when he won a CHOOSE**MATHS** excellence in teaching award.

He is the current editor of the Mathematical Association of Victoria's primary school journal, *Prime number*, and he presents at conferences around Australia.

Jess has been a classroom teacher at Moonee Ponds West Primary School (MPWPS) in Melbourne since 2012. MPWPS describes itself as child-centred with an emphasis on deep enquiry, critical thinking and creativity. She is currently the numeracy learning specialist for the school, a role that allows her to coach and mentor others whilst remaining in the classroom. Invested in improving teaching practice, Jess recently completed a Graduate Certificate in Primary Mathematics Education. She is also a regular contributor to *Prime number*.

Lucy is the Director of Taught Courses in the School of Education at the University of Nottingham. She has vast experience in the international education context, working with students (who are teachers) from all continents on a wide range of Masters level and doctoral programmes. Lucy started her career teaching English in Japan before completing her PhD at the University of Nottingham, which explored issues in language teaching. She is currently engaged in research in a range of schools around the world.

Tony is a writer and educational consultant. Previously he has been Head of the School of Education and Childhood at Leeds Beckett University; programme leader for the BA Primary Education at Nottingham Trent University; and course leader for the PGCE Mathematics at Nottingham University. His most recent publications include two books for Routledge: *Understanding and teaching primary mathematics* 4th Edition and *Teaching for mathematical understanding – Practical ideas for outstanding lessons*. He is the lead author for *Oxford international primary mathematics* and recently published *Approaches to learning and teaching primary: A toolkit for international teachers* for Cambridge University Press. He edits *Mathematics Teaching*, the journal of the Association of Teachers of Mathematics in the UK. He has worked with teachers and beginning teachers in 24 countries over the last 40 years and is currently working with the government of Belize to resource their new primary mathematics curriculum.

Helen almost dropped out of the teaching profession before she had begun, declaring to her university tutor that she could not be part of a discipline system which regularly caned children. The tutor reacted by suggesting she apply to teach in an innovative school on the outskirts of Sheffield which was totally different to any of the schools she had been placed in so far. This first exciting secondary school with the potential for cross-curricular teaching and a specific responsibility for developing drama 'within and without the curriculum' led to further teaching and support roles in both secondary and primary schools, where she used her expertise in teaching through the medium of experiential or process drama for many years. International experience began with a drama conference in Bosnia and continued with a cross-cultural project exploring anti-racist approaches to education, with teachers and academics in Prague, Copenhagen, Lisbon and Nottingham. Helen drew on this wide experience to lecture on education courses at three universities, including a bespoke retraining course at Leeds Metropolitan University, now Leeds Beckett, for teachers who had sought refuge and a new teaching role in the UK. Currently, Helen is an assistant professor on the PGCEi course at the University of Nottingham, working with cohorts in Bangkok since 2013.

The educators who will share their experiences

For this book we were joined by ten educators and two artists from around the world and worked closely with them in exploring their responses to teaching during the global pandemic. These educators are

Edward Emmett was born and educated in London, England. Currently lives and teaches at a school in Bangkok, Thailand. He teaches a Year 1 class.

Jasmine Irani is a member of the Teaching and Learning Collaboration (TLC). A multi-disciplinary team comprised of ABA (Applied Behaviour Analysis) Consultants, Supervisors and Tutors, Clinical Psychologists, Speech and Language and Occupational Therapists, based in London and the South East of England. She primarily supports individuals with special educational needs (SEN) and their families and the majority of her work is carried out face to face either 1:1 or in small groups in families' homes, schools and the community.

Seb Jefferies currently teaches at an international school in Ulaanbaatar, Mongolia, teaching English to grades 1–3. The school has always been progressive and keen to listen to the views of their teachers. He says that during the pandemic there has been constant discussion on how to best improve students' academic ability while paying careful attention to their social and emotional needs.

Shane Johnstone is an artist, sculptor and educator whose work primarily focuses on socially engaged models of practice. Formally an old school sign-writer and seaside fairground artist, latterly a muralist and street artist producing large-scale public works celebrating the working-class vernacular of Northern England, its expression, flamboyance and significance to our shared culture and heritage.

Amanda Queiroz Moura teaches at two schools in Sao Paulo in Brazil. She teaches engineers at a private college and teaches mathematics at a Catholic high school to predominantly middle-class students. She also supports PhD students at the University of Sao Paulo.

Nicodemus Amboko Muhati teaches History, and occasionally sociology and Swahili at Key Stage 3 and 4 at Braeside School, Nairobi, Kenya. Braeside is a co-educational international school, teaching students aged 3–18, and is part of the Braeburn Group of International Schools.

Betty Sheila Mumbi is a teacher of Humanities and PE. Her first degree was in Political Science and Sociology from the University of Nairobi, but she chose not to pursue politics but to work with students instead. She is currently working as a Graduate Assistant at St Andrew's, a Christian International boarding school in Turi, a town in the Kenyan Rift Valley, two to three hours north west of Nairobi.

Hubert Mathanzima Mweli is the Director-General at the Department of Basic Education, South Africa. He started life as a teacher in Bophirima High School in 1990.

Delmer Tzib is a History teacher in a high school in Belize. He studied history at the University of Belize and then spent two years in the South Pacific studying for a Masters. History teaching in Belize is fascinating as the curriculum includes African history, Mayan history and Caribbean history, all of which make up the history of Belize. Delmer teaches students between the ages of 13–18. The historical data he draws on creates lots of opportunities for debate.

Eddy (Edwina) Walton is currently Head of Department in a mainstream secondary school in Nottinghamshire, UK, and has worked with Helen and Tony with university sessions. She teaches Religious Education to 11–18 year-olds, with a focus on developing the whole person to be part of a responsible, inclusive global society. Eddy is not an artist but her love for creativity has influenced her work on this book and her teaching on a daily basis.

Louise Whyte is a secondary science teacher, teaching biology and chemistry at a British School in Valencia, Spain. It is a private school that teaches the British curriculum alongside the Spanish subject requirements, so students have a busy timetable. Louise has been teaching for ten years, three in the UK and seven in Spain, and enjoys developing practical and project-based learning activities.

Vicky Van Wyk has recently moved from Myanmar to Bangkok and is working with children who are five to six years old. She taught an online summer school programme in Bangkok but for this book describes her teaching during the early part of the pandemic in Myanmar with young children who have limited English skills.

You will notice that each chapter includes a graphical response to the issues raised and discussed in the chapter. Our previous book, *Being a teacher*, included this as a part of the analysis and many readers said that they found the graphical representations useful. We have developed this approach for this book. Eddy Walton, who provided the graphics for *Being a teacher* is again a part of the team. A new member of the contributing team, artist Shane Johnstone has also responded to the issues raised in the book. We asked him to read the text and respond in any way he felt appropriate. Many of you will have issues raised as you read the text, but, we also know, that many readers respond to graphics or images as a way of developing thinking and raising questions. That is why you see a range of images in the text. This is not a new idea, but perhaps it is a forgotten idea. Many European medieval texts contain what is usually called *marginalia*. These illustrations, which surrounded and often took over from the text, were integral to the ideas the authors of the texts were sharing. So, consider the images our contribution to the return of marginalia.

How we hope you use this book

There will be some of you reading this book as a library copy. Some of these copies may have been annotated by previous readers. You will have all read books where previous readers have underlined sections of text or added smiley faces at the side of a paragraph as a comment. I have even once had a book in which somebody had crossed out a large chunk of text and written 'This is ridiculous' in the margin. You may have heard of Fermat's theorem. The French mathematician, Pierre de Fermat, conjectured that there are no positive integers numbers a, b and c, which satisfy the equation $a^n + b^n = c^n$ for any integer value of n bigger than 2. (You may recognise the case for n = 2 being Pythagoras' theorem). Fermat stated this theorem as a note in the margin of a book called *The arithmetica* and added that he had found a beautiful proof of the theorem but that there wasn't space in the margin to write it down. Fermat jotted these notes down in 1637, but it wasn't until 1994 that an English mathematician, Andrew Wiles, finally proved the theorem. If only there had been more space in the margin of *The arithmetica*!

We would encourage you to annotate and jot in this book (buy a copy so that you don't have to take it back to an annoyed librarian). We would encourage you to add notes from other readings that you do that you feel resonate with the ideas we are sharing with you. In this way, you are turning this book into a *Commonplace book*. Such commonplace books were familiar to many in the 19th and early 20th centuries. These were more than diaries or journals. They include notes from everyday events but also would include cuttings from newspapers or journals, images that had been found and sketches of images that had engaged the author or copied out quotations.

You will notice that we have even made space for you to add jottings – Fermat would have had no problem with this layout. Take advantage of this space; use it in any way that you feel is appropriate. We would also encourage you to read the book collaboratively. Many people are members of reading groups or 'book clubs' so follow this approach. Read chapters with friends or colleagues so that you can discuss them. Make notes about these discussions in the book. Several readers contacted us to say how much they enjoyed being invited to write and draw in their copies of *Being a teacher*. They even suggested that it felt a little transgressive and so empowered them to try out other little acts of rebellion in their teaching. We hope you feel the same.

Tony's children understand his foibles and enthusiasms. Adam and Rachel, middle son and daughter-in-law gave him a book, *The booksellers tale*, by Martin Latham, for Christmas 2020. If you were to look in this copy you would see the following paragraph, a quotation from Henry Miller in his out-of-print book, *The books in my life*, underlined:

> In marginal annotations of books one can discover one's former selves. When one realizes the tremendous evolution of one's being, which occurs in a lifetime one is bound to ask … did I learn my lessons here on earth?

So, write away.

And finally …

We end our brief preface, as we did the preface to our previous book, by returning to bell hooks, who sums up the work of the fantastic educators that have worked on this book and celebrates the communities in which they work.

> When we commit ourselves to education as the practice of freedom, we participate in the making of an academic community where we can be and become intellectuals in the fullest and deepest sense of the word. We participate in a way of learning and being that makes the world more rather than less real, one that enables us to live fully and freely. This is the joy in our quest.
>
> (hooks, 1999 p72)

Further reading

Cooker, L., Cotton, T. and Toft, H. (2018) *Being a teacher: Teaching and learning in a global context*. Abingdon: Routledge.

This book, the predecessor to *Transforming teaching*, shares the stories of educators working in a diverse range of international contexts. We draw on personal narratives to explore effective teaching and learning in global settings to show how personal values influence pedagogical practice. The authors reflect on their experiences not just as teachers but also as learners, to offer guidance for prospective and current educational professionals.

hooks, b. (1994) *Teaching to transgress*. New York: Routledge.

bell hooks, who deliberately uses lower case in her name, shares her philosophy of the classroom in this book. She offers ideas about teaching that fundamentally rethink the ways in which we teach to support a new kind of democratic participation. She explains how she sees education as the practice of freedom.

hooks, b. (1999) *Talking back: Thinking feminist, thinking black*. New York: South End Press.

As with many of us, bell hooks was taught that 'talking back' meant daring to disagree or have an opinion when speaking to someone who saw themselves as having authority over her. In this book she reflects on how racism and feminism interacts with education. She suggests that moving from silence into speech is for all those who feel the oppressed, a gesture of defiance that heals, making new life and new growth possible, the very stuff of education.

Acknowledgements

We wanted to make space for all contributors to acknowledge everyone who had supported them over the last year or so. We have all faced challenges and seen the impact of the pandemic first-hand. We have all needed to draw on the strength of those that we hold dearest and have relied on the many people fighting the pandemic on the front line. Thanks to you all.

Tony would like to thank Felix and Tate, his two grandsons, aged eight and three when this book was written. They teach him more than anyone about how children learn mathematics, and kept him going through both periods of lockdown. The daily *Zoom* sessions were the highlight of every day. He would also like to thank Lucy for the amazing PGCEi course at the University of Nottingham and for being an inspirational colleague and friend. And, most of all, Helen. Without Helen nothing would make sense.

Jess would like to thank her incredible group of students from the year that was, the children of Room 17 in 2020. As learners and as people, they showed resilience, patience and empathy. She would also like to thank MM for the decade of inspiring mentorship and friendship.

Seb would like to thank his wonderful, intelligent and forever cheerful students! During their online lessons they have been inspirational in how they are able to adapt to change in these uncertain times and also bring a smile and a good attitude to each online lesson. Through their Google Meets they brought a much-needed slice of 'normal' during lockdown. Without them the whole PGCEi experience would have been impossible – it has been a privilege to reflect on my own practice through their learning. He would also like to thank his tutor Tony Cotton for his guidance through the whole PGCEi process.

Shane would like to thank Tony and Helen for introducing him to their world and all the other contributors for sharing their stories. Personal thanks to his daughter Campasme and granddaughter Arizona for the immense love and joy they bring and Sue for always being there.

Michael would like to thank Carla, Nash, Isaiah and Genevieve. Spending more time together was definitely the silver lining of 2020.

Betty would like to thank Ms Jane Holloway, Deputy Head Academics, St. Andrew's Prep School Turi, for her help and immense support as she started out teaching. Her guidance, support, and belief have seen her through the variability of teaching in a pandemic.

Helen thanks all her PGCEi students for developing her understanding of what it is to be truly internationalist in outlook. Sohm Kapila Senior and Amit Kapila for making a lifetime's dream of a trip to India come true just before Covid-19 hit the world. Thanda Gumede for teaching so much more than singing to her lockdown 'Singing for Pleasure' choir. Along with her amazing children Holly, Adam and Sam and their partners Ben, Rachel and Jasmine and of course grandchildren Felix, Tate and Quinn, who all join her in being centred by Tony.

Vicky would like to express her utmost gratitude to her sister Kathlene for her unparalleled love and support. Kathlene has always been her personal cheerleader and especially during these unprecedented times of the pandemic, has kept her spirits high. Without her, life would merely be a monotonous bus ride. Vicky would also like to thank Tony, who has been a wonderful mentor and inspiration. He has guided and challenged her to become a better educator and researcher, aspects which Vicky will always be grateful for.

Part I

Setting the scene

Chapter 1

Introduction

Everything has changed. We need to throw the book out of the window and write the new book.

(Vicky Van Wyk)

We live in changed times. Our usual ways of living our professional and personal lives have changed and the way everyone carries out their work has had to respond very quickly to government restrictions and advice. No matter where we live in the world, as the pandemic hit each country, working from home for many people became a new normal. The gap grew between those, mainly in professional occupations, who could work from home. Those in the caring sector, the construction sector or service sectors, who could not work from home, either lost their incomes or had to continue to take their chances with the virus. Whilst parents navigated these dramatic changes, teachers' and children's experience of school also changed overnight or with very little time to adjust.

Many of us are in our second, or even third, period of supporting our learners through home schooling, or at least out of the classroom schooling. Different countries learned different lessons, as we moved from one lockdown to the next. In some places, governments mandated amounts of time that teachers should remain online with their students, other countries worked with teachers and educators to find alternative platforms that could have a wider reach as they realised the inequity of relying on access to the internet for education. Bandwidth became synonymous with access to education in some countries.

School closures began on the 16 February. At this stage, UNESCO reports that 999 014 learners had been affected by changes to education, which amounted to 0.1% of all enrolled learners across the globe. There had been one country-wide closure at this point. Almost a month

DOI: 10.4324/9781003150596-1

after this, on the 24 March, the Victorian state government in Australia decided to close schools. By this stage 52.4% of all enrolled learners had been affected by restrictions and there were 145 country-wide closures.

By 1 April nearly 1.5 billion learners were affected, which is 84.3% of all enrolled learners. At this point there were 172 country-wide closures. This situation persisted well into June. In July and August, the virus seemed to be in retreat in many countries, but the impact of the virus seems to be returning as we move into September and October when this section is being written.

It seems worth noting that these figures refer to those engaged in education. Millennium goal 2 and target 2a was 'to ensure that by 2015, children everywhere, boys and girls alike, will be able to complete a full course of primary schooling'. The UN reports that in 2015, 57 million children of primary school age were out of school, with children from the poorest households four times as likely to be out of school as those from the richest households.

In the same way that access to education is impacted by poverty, the impact of the pandemic is also skewed towards the poorest in our world. The International Rescue Committee (IRC), a charity which supports people whose lives and livelihoods are shattered by conflict and disaster, reports that the pandemic could infect up to one billion people and kill 3.2 million people in 34 countries they identify as 'crisis affected countries', places where the virus can spread rapidly and where there is very limited access to medical facilities. They are particularly worried about countries like Bangladesh, which house the largest and most densely populated refugee camps in the world.

The CEO of the IRC, David Milliband, said, 'These numbers should serve as a wake-up call: the full, devastating and disproportionate weight of this pandemic has yet to be felt in the world's most fragile and war-torn countries' (see www.cnbc.com/2020/04/28/coronavirus-could-kill-more-than-3-million-people-in-vulnerable-and-poor-countries-aid-group-says.html).

To put this in context, the population of Africa is 1.2 billion and the current estimated population of the world's second-most populous city, Delhi, is 29.3 million people. So, this estimate suggests that the equivalent of the population of Delhi could die in the world's poorest 34 countries as a result of the pandemic.

Of course, Covid-19 is not the first virus or health emergency that the poorest in our world have faced. World Vision reports that over

11000 people died as a result of the West African Ebola outbreak in 2014. In 2018 there were an estimated 228 million cases of malaria worldwide, leading to over 400 000 deaths. Malaria deaths for children under five years old amount to 67% and 94% of malaria deaths occur in Africa. In 2018 the total funding for malaria control and elimination was US$ 2.7 billion. This contrasts to an estimated nine trillion dollars so far spent on fighting Covid-19.

The global educational response

The immediate response in most countries to try to halt the spread of Covid-19 was to close schools. The second response was to explore and develop ways that learning could move from face-to-face teaching and learning to learning being supported by virtual platforms or other forms of remote learning. One of the few countries to keep schools open was Sweden. A paper *Open schools, Covid-19, and child and teacher morbidity in Sweden* published in the *New England journal of medicine* found that there was a low incidence of severe Covid-19 among primary school children. It also found that the risks to teachers were lower than other groups. Sweden did however shift to distance learning for upper secondary education and higher education from mid-March 2020.

The decision to close schools in Australia was up to individual states. Despite the national cabinet's health advice for schools to remain open, Victoria, New South Wales, Queensland and the Australian Capital Territory (ACT) officially moved to remote learning at the beginning of Term 2, whilst other states implemented more individualistic approaches.

It would appear that the consistent response in most countries was to shut schools. However, no country that we have come across made any changes to the expected taught curriculum. Even though several countries cancelled national high stakes examinations, including Australia's controversial National Assessment Program- Literacy and Numeracy (NAPLAN), there does not seem to have been a move towards a long-term change in assessment regimes. It is, of course, the task of this book to explore these changes in some depth, so for this introduction let us just look at the International Baccalaureate (IB) and Cambridge International as exemplars of international education curricula.

The International Baccalaureate curriculum is used in over 5 000 schools in over 150 countries (source ibo.org) and their stated mission is to 'create a better world through education'. They built a microsite to support their schools and learners engaged with the IB. This site offered support, materials and resources to support remote learning as well as a community blog through which the IB community *could* share the stories of their responses to education under the pandemic. Much of the IB curriculum involves coursework, so examinations were cancelled and grades awarded reflected this coursework. The IB organisation also liaised with universities to try to smooth the path to students' chosen university even though the way in which grades were awarded had changed.

The Cambridge Assessment International Education (CAIE) claims to support 'early one million learners in 10 000 schools across 160 schools'. As with the IB organisation they provided resources to support remote learning and a series of professional development materials to help teachers. Neither the IB nor the CAIE made any changes to the curriculum requirements or have suggested any change to assessment requirements once schools have returned.

Whilst making no changes to the curriculum requirements as such, the Department of Education in Victoria listed three teaching priorities upon the return to face-to-face learning in Term 4. Having carried out the majority of the 2020 school year online, they identified mental health and well-being as the highest priority, acknowledging the potential negative impact of isolation and multiple transitions over the course of the school year. A learning focus with a concentration on literacy and numeracy was listed as the second priority, as a means to fill in potential gaps for those that may have been disadvantaged by remote learning. Being Term 4, transitions were named as the third priority, recognising those particular students facing critical milestones such as the move from Kinder to Foundation, Year 6 into Year 7 and those graduating from Year 12.

We are interested that it seemed to be a global fact that the curriculum should not be altered, only the way that the curriculum was accessed by learners. Some interviewees reported feeling very fearful prior to or at the beginning of their lockdown and many myths began to circulate about some of the platforms being used to teach in some countries. One educational response might have been to work with learners to reduce the number of myths that rapidly spread across social media and gained currency in many parts of the world. The World Health Organisation (WHO) lists some of these myths on their website (www.who.int). These myths include:

- Vitamin and mineral supplements can cure Covid-19
- Hydroxychloroquine has clinical benefits in treating Covid-19

- Wearing masks while exercising is dangerous
- Covid-19 can be spread on the soles of your shoes
- The prolonged use of masks can lead to oxygen deficiency
- Drinking alcohol protects you from Covid-19
- Adding pepper to your food prevents Covid-19
- House flies and mosquitos transmit Covid-19
- Drinking methanol, ethanol or bleach prevents Covid-19
- The virus is spread by 5G mobile networks
- Exposing yourself to the sun or temperatures higher than 25 degrees C, or taking a hot bath, protects you from Covid-19
- Cold weather and snow kills Covid-19

The WHO website carefully details the science behind the debunking of these myths and could easily have formed an interesting module in most science curricula.

International responses to education under the pandemic

Before we move into the particular stories about how the countries our co-authors work in responded, it is worth looking at an overview of the 12 countries in which we work. This is perhaps best seen as a table. The Blavatnick School of Government at the University of Oxford in the UK have developed a government response tracker which compiles data across 17 different indicators. This is updated and published online at covidtracker.bsg.ox.ac.uk.

This table collates the data from 14 October 2020. This should be seen as a snapshot as it captures the policy at the time the data was collated rather than an average over time. For example, on 14 October 2020 the schools were closed in Belize, Brazil and Myanmar but fully open in South Africa, Spain and Thailand.

	Maximum index	Australia	Belize	Brazil	Kenya	Mongolia	Myanmar	South Africa	Spain	Thailand	United Kingdom
School closing	100	67	100	100	67	33	100	0	0	0	33
Workplace closing	100	67	67	100	33	67	100	33	67	33	67
Cancel public events	100	100	100	100	100	100	100	50	100	50	100
Restrictions on gatherings	100	100	100	100	75	0	100	50	100	50	100
Close public transport	50	50	0	100	50	0	50	0	0	0	50

Continued

	Maximum index	Australia	Belize	Brazil	Kenya	Mongolia	Myanmar	South Africa	Spain	Thailand	United Kingdom
Stay at home requirements	100	67	33	67	33	0	100	67	33	33	33
Restrictions on internal movement	100	100	100	100	100	0	100	0	100	50	100
International travel controls	100	100	50	25	50	100	100	75	75	75	50
Income support	50	50	50	50	50	50	0	50	100	100	100
Debt/contract relief	100	100	100	50	50	100	0	100	100	100	100
Public information campaigns	100	100	100	100	100	100	100	100	100	100	100
Testing policy	100	100	67	67	100	67	67	100	67	67	67
Contact tracing	100	100	100	100	100	100	50	100	50	100	50

The table below shows how these policy decisions are currently impacting on the progress of the virus (compiled on 14 October 2020).

	Australia	Belize	Brazil	Kenya	Mongolia	Myanmar	South Africa	Spain	Thailand	United Kingdom
Total deaths	898	37	150 488	777	0	664	17 863	32 929	59	42 875
Deaths as % of population	0.0035	0.009	0.71	0.0014	Not available	0.0012	0.03	0.07	0.00008	0.06
Total tests	8 035 558	Not available	Not available	574 712	Not available	317 765	4 407 441	10 840 527	888 881	23 709 494
Tests as % of population	31	Not available	Not available	1	Not available	0.58	7.43	23	1.3	34

(The tables were compiled using https://worldhealthorg.shinyapps.io/covid/.)

This data, which is very crude as it relies on different forms of reporting from different countries, at best gives a broad sense of the impact of the pandemic at a national level. Broadly, it suggests that in terms of deaths the virus has had a much greater impact in Brazil, Spain and the UK than Belize and Thailand. This data only gives a glimpse of the impact of the virus and no sense of how the virus has affected the lives and educational experience of teachers and their students. That is the purpose of the second part of this book.

We introduced you to the idea of a commonplace book in the preface. We would invite you to pause in your reading at this point and reflect on your personal experience of the pandemic. The questions here mirror the questions that we asked each of the collaborating authors and asked ourselves at the start of the process.

Personal responses

> **Commonplace book: Entry 1**
>
> How has your day-to-day experience of education changed as a result of the pandemic?
>
> How have your relationships with key colleagues changed?
>
> How have your relationships between teachers and learners changed?
>
> How have the relationships between teachers and parents and the community changed?

10 Setting the scene

What might education be in a post-pandemic world?

In a sense this is the question that underpins the book. Exploring and sharing our experiences of the situation we all find ourselves in, we hope to explore how the purpose of education might be shifted in working through the current crisis.

By analysing our stories we can transform our shared vision of what learning and teaching might be in a post-pandemic world.

We want to finish this chapter with an image created by one group of participants in the Post Graduate Certificate of Education (International) (PGCEi) that we will teach on. In 'Creating visual explanations improves learning', Eliza Bobek and Barbara Tversky claim that 'there are several notable differences between visual and verbal explanations; visual explanations map thought more directly than words and provide checks for completeness and coherence as well as a platform for inference, notably from structure to process' (available at www.ncbi.nlm.nih.gov/pmc/articles/PMC5256450/).

We invite you to create your own image as a starting point on your journey exploring the purpose of education. And, as a corollary, what sort of learning experiences we should aim to provide.

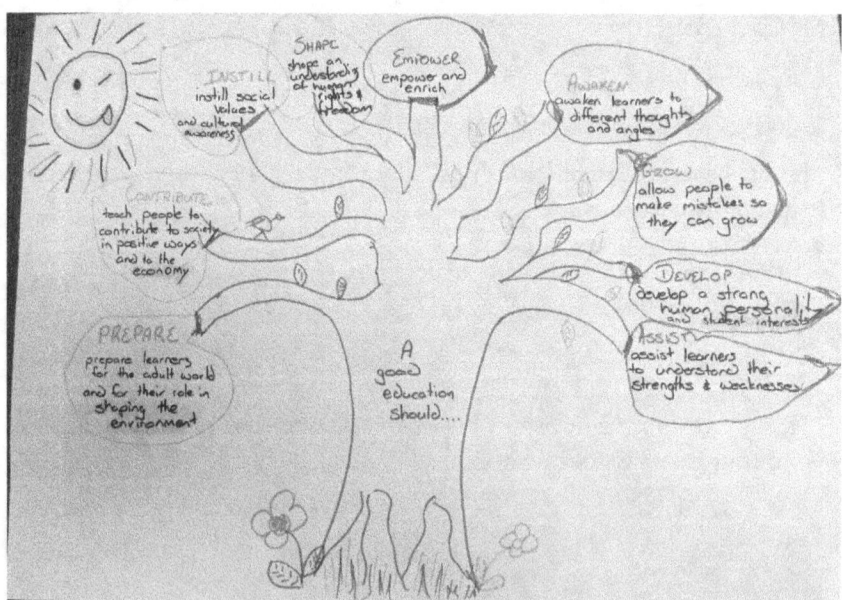

Introduction 11

Commonplace book: Entry 2

Create your own image to illustrate

A good education should....

Further reading

Bobek, E. and Tversky, B. (2016) Creating visual explanations improves learning, in *Cognitive research: Principles and implications*. Volume 1. No. 27. Published online 2016 Dec 7. doi: 10.1186/s41235-016-0031-6

The International Rescue Committee (IRC). www.rescue-uk.org

UNICEF. https://www.unicef.org/appeals/covid-19

World Health Organisation. (2020) Covid 19 explorer. Available online at https://worldhealthorg.shinyapps.io/covid

Chapter 2

Educational aims and values for the 21st century

Introduction

As we have suggested before, this book arose directly from the International Post Graduate Certificate of Education where Lucy, Tony and Helen originally met and currently teach on. The first module on the course is called 'Educational aims and values in international contexts'. This seems like an important issue for this book too. Our key aim for the book is to explore how learning and teaching might be transformed, for both learners and teachers, as a result of our experiences teaching under the pandemic. For the three of us the pandemic has reminded us of what lies at the heart of our passion for education, for learning and for teaching. When learning is rationed; when teaching is limited to virtual communication; when we are spending our time becoming accustomed to new technologies and learning platforms; we can forget why we were in the education business in the first place. Success becomes making contact because the wi-fi is working rather than whether or not anything educational happens as a result of that contact.

This chapter also serves to allow you, the reader, to notice what it is that you take for granted about your practice. It is very easy to slip into routines and rituals which are accepted norms in a particular school or country without wondering why we do things in the way that we do. We only notice this when we are faced with a very different way of doing things. We hope that the range of views we present in this chapter serve to help you notice what you currently see as 'common-sense' approaches which may, for others in different settings, seem far from common-sense. In this way your ears may be opened to the stories that make up the rest of the book.

DOI: 10.4324/9781003150596-2

Aims and purposes of education

As a starting point to the PGCEi, we ask all the participants to explore and interrogate their own values. One of the joys of teaching on a truly global course is the diversity of educational experience that the participants bring. This makes the discussion of aims and values deep and fruitful. Early in the course we ask participants to read a paper called *Why do we educate* by the British Columbia Teachers Federation. A quotation from the premier of British Columbia opens the paper. He says:

> Education has a whole bunch of roles. Ultimately education's role is to make sure that any citizen has the chance to lead the kind of fulfilling life that they want to lead, to be able to think for themselves, make good decisions, be good citizens and also go out and get a job.

It is worth noting that 'go out and get a job' comes at the end of this statement as an 'and also'. So often in government curricula the economy seems to take priority. The British Columbia education plan is then built around six core areas. The plan states that

We educate to

- Experience a good and worthwhile life
- Participate in community and democracy
- Respect diversity and difference
- Make a living
- Build and maintain positive relationships
- Care for the environment

We invite you to pause for a moment and think about both the stated aims of the school in which you work and how those aims are enacted in the curriculum. Could you see any of the aims above in your current classroom? How do you develop the skills needed to participate in community and democracy in your lessons?

A recent UNICEF publication, with the rather unwieldy title, *Research on child wellbeing, inequality and materialism* (available at www.unicef.org.uk/wp-content/uploads/2011/09/Child_Friendly_

Report060911-final-from-Ipsos.pdf), reports on research carried out with children from the UK, Sweden and Spain exploring what makes children happy. If one of our educational aims is experiencing a good and worthwhile life, then happiness and well-being seem to be important.

The report details what the children said made them happy. Children in all three countries said that 'Spending time with people they love (friends, family and even pets), being outdoors and doing fun activities' made them happy. The report says that children did not talk about material things making them happy and saw family time as the most important of all. Perhaps virtual learning has emphasised this. Material things took a backseat, well-being and health became all important. Family time became the norm when schools closed – maybe one measure of the success of virtual learning is how much we enabled families to engage.

In contrast children said that 'problems at home, fights with friends, being bullied and being bored and stuck indoors' made them unhappy. Again, this may have been exacerbated by learning at home. Children certainly became stuck at home, but you will read in the stories that make up the rest of this book how the teachers did their best to make sure children were not bored.

We would like to invite you to annotate this book with your aims and values. Why do you educate? Use the box below to either list your aims for education with examples of how you do this or use a graphic to illustrate your aims.

Commonplace book entry

I educate so my learners can ...

Purposes of teaching

Paul Ernest, a mathematics educator and philosopher explored the different perspectives that teachers will bring to the classroom. He explored this in acknowledgement that different people and different systems will see alternative purposes for education. This is not to say there is a single 'correct' purpose for teaching; rather, that it is useful to be able to analyse classroom practice against these different aims and purposes. It can also help explain the tensions that teachers often feel in terms of what is possible in their classroom. If there is a clash between personal aims and the aims of the school or the state this can lead to feelings of frustration. He first posed these aims in *The philosophy of mathematics education* published in 1991. The whole book is available at https://p4mriunpat.files.wordpress.com/2011/10/the-philosophy-of-mathematics-education-studies-in-mathematicseducation.pdf.

He recently developed these ideas in the article *Ethics and the mathematics teacher* in *Mathematics teaching 266*, published in May 2019. He calls the categories below interest groups. The article goes on to explore the implications of each interest group for the learners in their classrooms. You might teach in another subject area, but we have still have left a blank space beneath each interest group for you to reflect on whether you feel that this aim resonates or conflicts with your own aims. It is also worth reflecting on the same question with regard to the school and the education system within which you work. The five interest groups are discussed below.

Industrial trainers

Acquiring basic mathematical skills and numeracy, and social training in obedience (authoritarian, basic skills-centred aims).

My aims	School aims	System-wide aims

Technological pragmatists

Learning basic skills and learning to solve practical problems with mathematics and information technology (industry and work-centred aims).

My aims	School aims	System-wide aims

Old humanists

Understanding and capability in advanced mathematics, with some overall appreciation of mathematics (pure mathematics-centred aims).

My aims	School aims	System-wide aims

Progressive educators

Gaining confidence, creativity and self-expression through mathematics (child-centred progressivist aims).

My aims	School aims	System-wide aims

Public educators

Empowerment of learners as critical and mathematically literate citizens in society (empowerment and social justice aims).

My aims	School aims	System-wide aims

Mike Bottery explored teaching in a similar way in his book *The morality of the school: The theory and practice of values in education* published by Cassell. You will notice the cross-over between his five purposes for education and those of Paul Ernest above. The five purposes of, or beliefs about education that Bottery identified, are cultural transmission; child-centredness; social reconstructionist; gross national product code and ecological. In short, education can be seen as a way of passing on a national culture from one generation to the next; is a way of empowering children to learn what is important to them; is a way of educating to change society for the better and/or is to enable a country to compete economically or is to save the planet.

These aims and beliefs will compete in schools on occasions. The same will apply to state curricula and in individual classrooms. On occasions differing aims will work together. One way to interrogate these aims is to try and view them from two opposing viewpoints. What is offered below is a conversation between the differing viewpoints for each belief.

Cultural transmission

- Education is an important vehicle for passing on cultural heritage to the younger generation. Teachers are guardians of this cultural heritage and they must pass this on to our pupils. Otherwise, our cultural heritage and our shared values will disappear.
- *But this is such a conservative ideology. Shouldn't we be more critical about our cultural heritage? To say 'we did it in this way in the past so we should do it in the same way now' is not socially progressive. It does not reflect how society will be in the future.*

Child-centred

- The child's interests and experiences must be central to learning. We all know children learn best when they are active and involved. Learning primarily takes place through child-initiated activity. The teacher should be a facilitator of learning and not simply an instructor.
- *But in allowing children to develop naturally, are we limiting them to their own interests? Is the focus on individuals an abdication of social responsibility? Could each child become a law unto herself or himself?*

Social reconstructionist

- Education is the best vehicle for societal change. The teacher has to be a facilitator rather than an instructor and should become a critical guide. This means they are a guardian of some values from the past and critical of other values. In their classroom the child is active and develops a critical identity through social interaction.
- *Isn't it too much to ask the teacher to be a social reformer and does a teacher have the moral right to do this? Might not valuable aspects of your cultural heritage be neglected in the passion for social reconstruction?*

GNP code

- Surely the primary purpose of education is to provide a well-trained workforce which can compete in the world economy. The teacher is both a trainer and a transmitter. Pupils must be able to fit into the economic system of the country. There is no point in pupils having initiative if it doesn't help them get a job.
- *But doesn't this narrow the curriculum? Surely education should prepare pupils for a life which involves more than just the economy and it must involve some criticism of an economy-driven model?*

Ecological

- Humanity is just one participant in the Earth's ecosphere, rather than being its ruler or exploiter, so if this ecosphere is not sustainable, then neither is humanity. Understanding how to achieve such sustainability, and the actions that derive from this, must then be critical educational aims.
- *Just as GNP education narrows the curriculum towards one which is economy-driven doesn't ecological education narrow it towards an environmental emphasis? How can humanity progress economically, socially and culturally, if we are all 'saving the world'?*

We invite you to use this diagram to reflect on these five beliefs. Use and label each sector for each belief and respond in any way you feel fit.

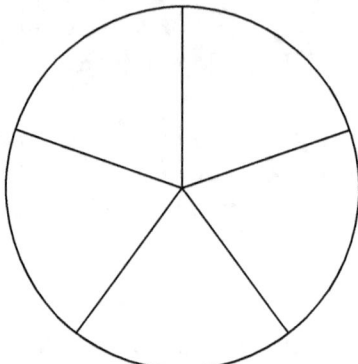

We would like to end this section by quoting Paul Ernest at some length. This is how he ends the piece we opened this section with. After analysing the different purposes for education, he decides that the key to successful teaching is care. He says:

> It may sound idealistic, but I believe the secret of outstanding teaching is care. Caring is a deep commitment to another person, the student in this case: caring about how they feel; about what interests them; about how best to support them in their present efforts and their future ambitions. It involves talking to and listening to each student to uncover their passions, curricular or extra-curricular and helping them to fulfil their dreams.

Which seems to bear a strong resemblance to the families that the children who were interviewed by UNICEF want to spend time with.

We said earlier in this chapter that one of the great joys about working with teachers from around the world is the range of viewpoints and experiences that they bring. The next section of this chapter looks at three of these viewpoints.

Alternative viewpoints

Another report that we ask the participants on the PGCEi to read is *Learning to read the world: Through other eyes* by Vanessa Andreotti and Lynn Mario de Souza. This forms an online study programme which allows participants to engage with indigenous perceptions of global issues. This indigenous view of education can open our eyes, as educators, as to the possibilities in our classrooms by allowing us to see different viewpoints as to what is important in educating.

The course follows a process which is similar to the process we have gone through in working on the book. The authors suggest that a starting point for our development as teachers is to notice what we take for granted in our practice and 'unlearn' it by understanding the social, cultural and political context in which this understanding was formed. We then need to listen to alternative viewpoints and use these to question our current practices. With this new understanding we can now explore ways that we can change our own professional practice.

The report explores four areas – development, education, equality and poverty. We recommend exploring the whole course, but for the purposes of this book we will just focus on education. Here are five alternative perspectives on education taken from the report.

Mereana Taki Rotorua Aontearoa (New Zealand)

In my language there is just one word for learning and teaching: AKO. The education that matters most is that which happens in your community. My role as a tribal adult is to apprentice my children into adulthood. I need to teach them about life in all its aspects – as it is unfolding. And how are they going to learn that if they are taken somewhere else and cannot see what I am doing? I used to take them with me everywhere, including to my work at the university. This caused a lot of problems to the mainstream system.

Dennis Banda (Zambia)

We have an African saying that it takes an entire village to educate a child. And when this child receives western-oriented schooling education, he or she meets contradictions between the school and what the community offer. He or she learns to navigate and negotiate through the school and community cultures all the time. At school the message is alternative knowledge to school knowledge is ignorance. The child finally becomes a stranger to her or his own community. Our elders have come up with an acronym for this schooling education. It is PHD – Permanent Head Damage.

Noemi Valle Sagrado (Peru)

The teachers in the village school taught me to read, to write and to count and then I left because they did not respect or value the ways of my people. They wanted everyone to live and think like the people in the city. What I learned of most value to me, I learned from my grandparents: to respect this land and to survive in it with integrity. Now I am attending a new college that respects our way of thinking.

Bob Randall Mutitjulu (Australia)

Some people come here and want us to change into what they have in mind we should be; others come and want us to stay the same. Neither consider that we need access to the resources of the dominant culture, but we have the right to decide what to do with it.

Bronwyn Thurlow Otautahi Aotearoa (New Zealand)

Education is more about bringing the person out than putting stuff (knowledge) in. In early childhood, education is about respectfully keeping out of the way to observe with awe and wonder, to allow holistic unfolding of the person, once the basics of physical care are taken care of. Who is this person? Where and who did they come from? Who will they become? What part is it my privilege to play?

We would invite you to use this blank space to reflect on one of these perspectives. In what ways does it challenge your current perspective on education?

Alternative perspectives

An educator who has influenced Tony and Helen greatly is Munir Fasheh. They attended a conference at which he was a keynote speaker and were lucky enough to spend time with him throughout the conference. Munir describes himself as a healed teacher and educator and works for the Arab Education Forum in Palestine. In his keynote address to the conference (which can be found in the journal *Mathematics teaching* issues 250 and 251) he introduced the participants to the Arabic ideas of *Mujaawarah*, *Yuhsen* and *Muthanna*. These ideas are at the heart of his conception of education.

Mujaawarah is any group of people who meet regularly together in order to learn. Such a group meets freely with no internal or external authority. The group develops wisdom as a group. There is no curriculum or assessment. At this point can we suggest a thought experiment? If there was no curriculum that you had to follow; if there were no examinations that you had to prepare your learners for; if the learners did not have to attend your classes, what would you teach?

Yuhsen can be seen as a measure of a person's worth. It could also be seen as a measure of the success of an education system. *Yuhsen* is measured in five ways:

- How well does a person use their technical knowledge?
- How beautiful or pleasing are the results of someone using their skills?
- How valuable to the community are the results of someone using their skills?
- How much does a person give of themselves to learning?
- How respectful of others is a person in discussions?

How differently might we view the curriculum if this was how it was assessed?

Finally, *Muthanna* refers to the relationship between teacher and learner. Munir suggests that this can best be described by the mathematical sentence $1 + 1 = 3$, which means that the sum of the two individuals is greater than the two individuals. The '3' stands for the new person that is formed through the relationship between teacher and learner when each individual is both learner and teacher.

For the final part of this chapter, we would like to briefly explore global skills and competencies. Many international schools see the development of such skills as something that can be offered.

Global skills and competencies

Sometimes called global skills and sometimes skills for the 21st century, this chapter explores in detail how the skills of communication and collaboration; creativity and critical thinking; intercultural competence and citizenship; emotional self-regulation and well-being and digital literacies came to be defined. It shows how they have been developed from educational theory.

Oxford University brought together an expert panel to write a position paper discussing these five global skills and competencies. The full paper is available at https://cdn.theewf.org/pdf/oup-expert-global-skills.pdf?mtime=20200106143256.

They share a range of frameworks for global skills and we would like to share three of these with you. As you explore each framework, you might like to reflect on the extent to which the setting in which you work could be seen as working within the framework.

The first is *UNESCO's four pillars of wisdom*. These are the 'pillars of education' that UNESCO suggests can form the basis of an education which can empower learners to reshape the world in which they live. The four pillars are:

Learning to know: Learning how to learn in order to better understand the complexity of the world.
Learning to do: Learning how to participate in the global economy and in society.
Learning to live together: Developing an understanding of their own culture and other cultures and understanding how we live interdependently.
Learning to be: Learning how to take responsibility for our own actions. How to act with autonomy, judgement and responsibility.

The second framework is the Organisation for Economic Cooperation and Development (OECD) Global Competence Framework developed with the Programme for International Student Assessment (PISA), the organisation which carries out the international comparison surveys. Rather than skills and competencies this model refers to four interrelated capacities which can be developed through the teaching of 'skills, knowledge, values and attitudes'.

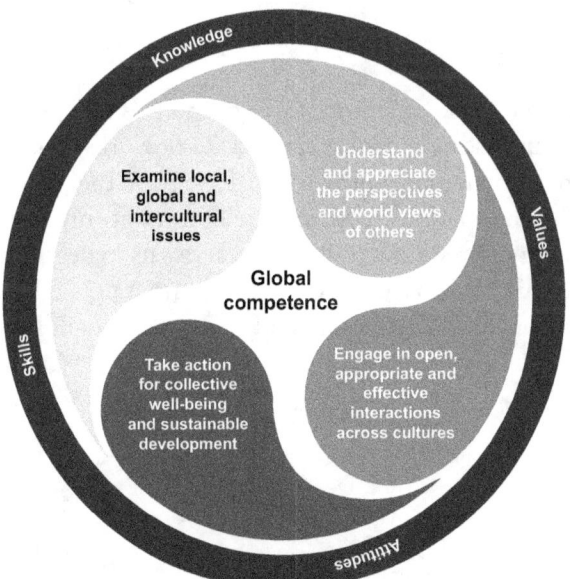

From PISA https://www.oecd.org/pisa/pisa-2018-global-competence.htm

A third framework comes from the University of Melbourne and is called the Assessment and Teaching of 21st Century Skills (ATC21s). Their framework comes in the form of a grid highlighting both ways of thinking, pedagogical approaches and outcomes.

WAYS OF THINKING	TOOLS FOR WORKING
• Creativity and innovation • Critical thinking, problem-solving, decision-making • Learning to learn/metacognition (knowledge about cognitive processes)	• Information literacy • Information and communication technology (ICT) literacy
WAYS OF WORKING	**WAYS OF LIVING IN THE WORLD**
• Communication • Collaboration (teamwork)	• Citizenship - local and global • Life and career • Personal and social responsibility – incluidng cultural awareness and competence

For further detail please see: Binkley, M., Erstad, O., Hermna, J., Raizen, S., Ripley, M., Miller-Ricci, M., & Rumble, M. (2012). Defining Twenty-First Century Skills. In Griffin, P., Care, E., & McGaw, B. Assessment and Teaching of 21st Century Skills, Dordrecht, Springer.

Final thoughts

As we suggested at the opening of this chapter, we hope that the range of aims and purposes for education and frameworks around which we can develop a curriculum allows you to notice the current restraints under which you operate. Noticing the constraints under which we all teach and being offered new possibilities allow us to begin the process of change. Use this final space to write down three possibilities for action in your own practice that you could make as a result of reading this chapter.

Possibilities for action

I will make the following changes to my practice:

1.

2.

3.

Further reading

Andreotti, V. and Mario de Souza, L. (2007) *Learning to read the world: Through other eyes*. Derby: Global Education. Available as a PDF from https://www.researchgate.net/publication/236003559_Through_Other_Eyes_learning_to_read_the_world

This report was produced by international partners, and is a four-part study programme, addressing the underlying values, assumptions that often remain unaddressed in global citizenship and development education. It is designed to be used to support individual or group study.

Bottery, M. (1990) *The morality of the school*. London: Cassell.

Mike Bottery explores how values impact and influence curriculum and teaching both at a strategic and at a classroom level.

British Columbia Teachers Federation. (2014) *Why do we educate*. Available as a downloadable PDF from https://eric.ed.gov/?id=ED573418

The paper asks critical questions regarding the role of education such as, 'Is it to make a living or to build a better world? To serve the needs of industry or to build a democratic society? Should the "educated citizen" be a critical thinker? A person who lives in a sustainable way and cares for the environment? An entrepreneur? Some of these? All of these? Something else altogether'?

Ernest, P. (1991) *The philosophy of mathematics education*. London: Taylor and Francis.

This book offers a model of five educational ideologies, each with its own epistemology, values, aims and social group. It explores the questionable assumptions, values and interests upon which much curriculum design is founded. The book finishes on an optimistic note, however, arguing that pedagogy is the way to achieve the aims of educating confident problem posers and solvers who are able to critically evaluate the social uses of mathematics.

Chapter 3

The contributors and the settings in which they work

Introduction

As we (Lucy, Tony and Helen) began planning this book we first discussed the authors we had previously worked with on *Transforming teaching*. As we would be working quickly to put the book together, we realised we should spread the web more widely. We were determined to include a wide geographical spread and to make sure we had male and female voices and stories from a range of ethnicities and backgrounds. As we began to make contact with possible writers, we were excited by the enthusiasm with which the project was greeted. There were people out there who thought it was as important as we did. When we started the interviews, the excitement grew and became palpable. We knew there was an important book in the making and in the writing.

So, whose stories will you be sharing as you read this book? Which of the authors might you connect with most; whose stories might you find most compelling? We hope that there will be moments as you read the book when you find that something resonates so much with your personal story you will shout, 'Yes'. We would encourage you to write 'Yes' in the margin and underline these sections. As we suggested earlier, we think it is important to annotate as you read. We hope that there are times when you disagree with something. We would ask you to stop at this point and try and work out why you disagree with this point in particular. Again, annotate the text.

Enjoy getting to know us all as you read this chapter. We hope you begin to make connections both with the authors as individuals and with the experiences that the authors share.

DOI: 10.4324/9781003150596-3

Lucy Cooker

I am the Director of Taught Courses in the School of Education at the University of Nottingham. In that role, I oversee all our postgraduate and undergraduate programmes. In addition, I tutor on the PGCEi, the international course about which you have read, and which spawned this book, and the Masters course in education, which is a flexible course. I also supervise Masters, Doctoral and PhD students. In addition to these roles I am the Director of Global Engagement for the Faculty of Social Sciences at the university, working with colleagues in the Faculty to develop networks and partnerships with individuals and organisations outside of the UK.

Just before the pandemic hit the UK my parents moved to my town, which was not as a result of Covid-19; it was a planned move. But, as a result of Covid-19, I have been more actively caring for them than I would otherwise have been, shopping and feeling I ought to see them every day. This is quite a big shift for me as previously they lived two hours' drive away, and I only saw them every six weeks or so.

I really enjoy my new role at the university. From March I had just been thinking about moving the PGCEi online. Now in this new, wider role I try to make lives as stress free as possible. I had to get my head round it all really quickly. Whole new courses, whole new systems, overseeing undergraduate courses which I had never run before, not teaching on them but learning new regulations and running examination boards for the first time. There were many sudden staff changes to deal with, many as a result of the changes due to the pandemic. All these changes came at the same time; it has been a big learning curve.

Tony Cotton

I work in a shed in my garden in Otley, near Leeds, in the UK. I combine work on the PGCEi Bangkok cohort for the University of Nottingham, with work as a textbook writer for the OUP (Oxford University Press) and Macmillan. As part of that work, I am frequently called upon to offer teacher education sessions and webinars to teachers in locations as diverse as Mexico, India and Belize. It has been fascinating how this side of my work has developed under the pandemic. Recently I found myself talking to over 250 teachers from 84 different countries, including the Ukraine, Iran, Iraq, Turkey, Saudi Arabia and other countries, which I might have found it difficult to travel to. In some ways this makes the webinars more inclusive. Any teacher with access to the internet or whose school has access to the internet could attend. I am sure that this is something that will develop even more in the post-pandemic future.

In addition, I am the editor of *Mathematics Teaching*, the journal of the Association of Teachers of Mathematics (ATM). We have already published a special issue looking at how teachers have responded to teaching remotely with articles written by teachers from all around the world. I also write a weekly blog post, engaging mathematics teachers in their continuing professional development.

I combine this variety of work with the important task of helping to look after my three young grandsons: Felix, Tate and Quinn. During the first lockdown that the UK experienced from March to June 2020, I ran online teaching sessions teaching for Felix and his friends. I am particularly interested in the ways that children learn mathematics outside of school and the differences between how that learning takes place compared to school learning. Using mathematical vocabulary naturally in everyday life (such as using 'dodecahedron' instead of '12 sided shape') and enabling children to spend time using that learning in everyday ways – playing with construction blocks, for example, shows children how to visualise and how to construct, and how big or small objects need to be to fit together. These are useful skills and will be useful at school and beyond. I have found myself recently drawing on this experience in my weekly blogs. I am learning a lot about how children learn from watching and working with Felix and Tate.

Edward Emmet

I am a primary Year 1 teacher from London working in a school situated in Nongprue, Thailand on the eastern Gulf coast known for its beaches. I have also worked as a nursery leader, reception teacher and an early years keystage coordinator. The school teaches the English and Welsh curriculum with an emphasis on a Montessori approach in the early years.

Each homeroom class has a lead teacher and several teaching assistants depending on the number of students in each class and the needs of the pupils. There are a range of nationalities represented within the homeroom teachers, including British, American, Canadian and Australian teachers. The assistants in the early years are of Thai nationality and in primary and secondary school are of Thai or Filipino descent. As well as the homeroom classes there are specialist subject teachers who teach Physical Education, Swimming, Art, English as a Second Language (ESL), Information and Communication Technology (ICT), Chinese, and Thai. The students are mainly either Thai or of shared Thai and Western heritage; however, there are several students from South Korea, India, England, Australia, America, Russia, China and Argentina.

In my spare time, I like to work on my own professional development, learning about different learning philosophies, especially those connected to a Montessori approach. I also take weekly drumming and singing lessons and with the skills I have learned I try to incorporate this into my current teaching practice. The school also places a big importance on sport and I support the school football teams with coaching. To help staff morale we have a teacher's football team that competes in the local 7-a-side football league. When I worked with the team that wrote *Being a teacher*, I was leading the early years department in a privately owned international school in Bangkok, but after four months off work for knee surgery, I have returned to just teaching one Year 1 class (five- to six-year-old learners) with no extra responsibilities while my knee heals. Early years teaching here is based on the Montessori method and needs adults who can play on their hands and knees, out of the question for me for at least 18 months.

There has been a lot to adjust to; there is much less play-based learning in Year 1 than I was used to in the early years setting. The structure of the school day is the same; I arrive at school at 8.15, start teaching at 9 with literacy, reading and mathematics all before lunch. Then my class has 'specialist' subjects in the afternoon including Thai, Chinese, physical education, information technology and, whatever the current topic is, religious education and science. I am having to get used to the limited use of Montessori materials in Year 1 and there is not much breathing space as we have to cover a vast array of learning objectives. As a result, our children have little free play time.

Jessica Greenbaum and Michael Minas

We both worked in the same school and that is how we met. I (Jess) teach Year 3 and 4 children (ages seven to eight) and have recently become the mathematics specialist. I have been a classroom teacher for eight years and this year took on the role of numeracy learning specialist. This means I get to visit classrooms across the school to support planning, to observe and support teaching, and I also carry out some coaching of teachers.

The school is in a reasonably affluent suburb of Melbourne in Victoria, Australia. There are about 500 students in the school, most from families with two working parents. This has proved interesting in terms of remote learning values. Quite a few parents hope that the remote learning materials will occupy their children rather than involve them in working with their children.

The school is seen as having progressive values and a socially conscious approach. The students are taught in multi-age classrooms; wearing the school uniform is optional and many students elect not to (which is unlike most Australian schools) and the students call their teachers by their first names. This is also unusual for Australian schools. Student choice and student voice is valued in the school. For example, there is one hour set aside each week where students can choose what they want to learn and where they will learn it. So, if a Year 2 student wants to play a board game with their Year 6 sibling, they can go to the Year 6 classroom to play the game.

As students of different ages are taught together rather than grouped around grade levels some students are barely aware of what year level they are in. They are all treated as individuals. Play-based learning is valued and evident throughout the school. Young students learn social skills very early in their school career through play. The school has a strong history of community events and does not lock the gates at the weekend. Although, I would have to admit that the school has become a little less community based recently. I wonder if this is because of the pressures of work on many of the parents.

I (Michael) taught at this school until very recently and I have been in education for over 20 years. I started as a support teacher for learners with additional needs when I was training to become a teacher. I then worked as a classroom teacher for 17 years in various primary schools. For the last couple of years, I have taught part time whilst setting up my own consultancy business in mathematics education. I am now a full-time consultant, working with schools on developing their approach to teaching mathematics. It has been an interesting time to start a new business as a consultant, although my *YouTube* channel www.youtube.com/channel/UC-F-4IIfKSd3mZCjs1zwukA/in which I share mathematical games designed for remote learning has proved very popular around the world during the various lockdowns.

Jasmine Irani

I am an Applied Behaviour Analysis (ABA) therapist working primarily with children and young people with Autism Spectrum Condition (ASC). I am based in Brighton. I work as both a supervisor and senior tutor and have recently taken on a trainee consultant position. This means that as well as direct face-to-face work, with children and young people, I am also involved in assessment; programme development; the training of other tutors and parent support. I am also a partner of the learning collective I work with, the Teaching and Learning Collaboration (TLC), which means I wear many 'hats' alongside my face-to-face teaching, mentoring other tutors, organising training and general administration. As well as accumulating supervision hours I am currently studying for the Board Certified Behaviour Analyst (BCBA) examination which I hope to take next year.

In a wider context I enjoy being a part of my community, volunteering as a cook for our local Casserole Club (a volunteer project aimed at reducing loneliness and food poverty amongst vulnerable people) and helping organise our community advent calendar. For this, a different street lights up their windows each day of advent. Living in Brighton means I can spend lots of time by the sea. I love swimming in the summer although I am not yet brave enough to do it in the winter. I also enjoy running along the seafront. Excitingly, me and my partner Sam have also recently got a puppy called Nancy who is brilliant, and funny, and teaching me lots of things. A definite highlight of an otherwise very strange year.

My normal working week varies depending on who I am working with. I often work with one child in their home with a programme of activities to suit their special needs. These sessions vary, say for a three-year-old I might work with them for two hours. All play-based and aimed at developing communication skills, learning to learn skills and age-appropriate daily living skills. There is a lot of flexibility, drawing on a range of activities and the child's own motivations and interests working towards identified targets through play. Then, I might be working with an older child who is home schooled full time. We have both academic targets to meet, with the addition of activities to develop the daily living skills he finds difficult. He also has physiotherapy, occupational therapy and language development sessions according to his needs at the time.

I also co-run after-school groups, such as 'Social Detectives', which is aimed at learners with ASC but can be for anyone who might benefit. 'Cadets' is for younger children and runs on Saturday mornings. I pop in and supervise this really lovely group run by other therapists who I support. There is also a really cool youth group that I sometimes go along to run conversation activities. This is more informal, tends to operate on an *ad hoc* basis and was set up by a parent's support group with our help. They invite leaders to offer music and art activities. It does help to be flexible in my work times. I do some after school and weekend groups, but I also try to keep most weekends precious.

Sebastian Jefferies

I have been in Mongolia for two years and I teach in a private international school for local children. There are very few *ex pat* children in the school. The parents of the students at the school are locals with a relatively high income as the fees for the school are higher than the average annual wage in Mongolia. So, we have children of celebrities such as pop stars; children of artists, children of engineers who work for mining firms or even children of owners of the mines. There are children whose parents are in finance or chief executives of large companies. There are several parents who have successfully set up their own start-ups. All these parents do different things but they all want their children to be successful.

Success for these parents includes studying abroad, to gain access to universities in the UK or the US. This means that a focus on learning English is really important. I think the expectation is that the students will return to Mongolia after studying to develop it as a country but sometimes being a doctor in the US appeals more than being a doctor in Mongolia.

Before the pandemic, school would run from 8.30 to 4.30. The students learn in Mongolian and English which is really mentally taxing. Every day is bilingual. Each day started with listening to the national anthem; sometimes there would be an awards ceremony or a student would perform on a traditional Mongolian instrument. These communal starts to the day are seen as very important.

I teach grades 2 and 3 and kindergarten in the afternoons. The lessons are very active; there is an emphasis on learning through doing. This is the expected pedagogical approach throughout the school which leads to the school being seen as progressive for Mongolia. In the state sector there is a lot of careful note taking from the board and a lot of sitting still. There is not very much active learning at all in the state schools.

Amanda Queiroz Moura

I came straight from classes and lunch to talk to you today. It is winter in Sao Paulo, very warm in the day but very cold at night. I work in two institutions: a college for engineers and a school for the children of people with more money than the average. In my research, I have a real concern about the quality of education in the public schools. These are for children of those parents without the money to pay for education. I recently finished my PhD and now help supervise research students for the academics who were my supervisors. When I was studying for my PhD I lived in Chicago, US, for a while to help my research.

The school I teach in is a Catholic school and I have students from traditional middle-class parents. Usually, classes start in January or February, but I started with my new class in March. My very first day in school was the first time the district was locked down. I have never met my students face to face because for all high schools the Secretary of Education in Sao Paulo said we should give a holiday for teachers to make plans for work during the pandemic. So, only one week after I started my school I started a one month vacation to prepare for online classes.

Nicodemus Amboko Muhati

I teach History, and occasionally sociology and Swahili at Key Stage 3 and 4 at Braeside School, Nairobi, Kenya. Braeside is a co-educational international school, teaching students aged 3–18, and is part of the Braeburn Group of International Schools. I am driven by the burning desire to be part of a positive social change that the world desires to achieve. I believe teaching is potentially the way to help contribute to the realisation of this change.

Why teaching? Teachers have the greatest influence on the lives of millions of young people in their generation, and by extension, to the whole society. Any decision and action done by a teacher in a classroom has got such high potential. I strongly believe that an education that is values based and transformational oriented is the best possible remedy to the challenges of today and tomorrow. I look at education as a social investment on the young generation. Each morning that I take a step into the classroom to teach History, I am motivated by the thought and understanding, that as a teacher, I have the opportunity to nurture and mentor future leaders; and an opportunity to cultivate not only the intellectual potentials of my students, but also their different talents and capabilities.

Betty Sheila Mumbi

I am a teacher of Humanities and PE. My first degree was in Political Science and Sociology from the University of Nairobi, but I chose not to pursue politics but to work with students instead. I am currently working as a Graduate Assistant at St Andrew's, a Christian International boarding school in Turi, a town in the Kenyan Rift Valley, two to three hours north west of Nairobi.

I teach in the Prep School, working with young children, although I trained to teach students of high school age. I teach children from reception to age eight and find it a challenge to teach younger students the basic skills they need for PE, such as balls skills, athletics, competitive games and swimming. In comparison, the older students already have those basic skills. I find the younger children get things wrong more frequently, but they are excited to learn and excited they're getting things wrong, but they are so excited to do it.

In Kenya schools closed abruptly. The announcement was made on a Sunday evening with the Ministry of Education sending out a notice to all schools that by the following Wednesday all schools had to be closed. This gave very little time to prepare for virtual learning and teachers had to adapt very fast. My school is a full boarding school with students from different countries so as ensuring all kids could get home, booking flights for them and making other travel arrangements, as well as making sure they had work as soon as they got home the learning could continue, was a very challenging task.

Hubert Mathanzima Mweli

I am the Director-General (DG) of Basic Education in the South African government. I assumed this position on 15 August 2015 and I have just been re-appointed for the second term as the DG of Basic Education.

I have a number of qualifications which include a Bachelor of Arts in Education with Honours, a Bachelor of Administration in Industrial Relations with Honours and a Master's Degree in Development and Management. I have occupied various positions in the public service and civil society. Before being appointed to my current position, in August 2015, I served, inter alia, as the Head of Department of the North West Education Department, the Deputy Director-General for Curriculum Policy, Support and Monitoring, and the Administrator of the Eastern Cape Education Department where I would like to think I impacted education positively. I have led delegations and missions to attend and present at a number of global events on behalf of the sector and the country. I think this experience, and the expertise I gained while holding these portfolios, have equipped me to serve as efficiently as I can, in leading Basic Education in South Africa.

I take the role of monitoring and supporting provinces, districts and schools very seriously. To support this, I set up engagements and visits to all the provincial and district officials as well as school principals in each of the regions. I do believe that what gets measured and monitored gets done. I have been part of a team which has seen a steady increase in the improvement of learning outcomes and the introduction of skills and competencies for a changing world in the South African curriculum and I think we have established a world-class curriculum and public examination system.

Helen Toft

My main job is teaching the PGCEi course at the University of Nottingham, which is where Tony and I met Lucy. Tony and I both work from home in northern England, Tony in the shed while I use the garden room or bedroom office. I am also a granny to an eight-year-old and a three-year-old with another grandson, a lockdown baby, due on 24 December, who we look after regularly. The rest of my day-to-day responsibility is caring for my 88-year-old mum, trying to make lockdown as pleasant as possible for her and others like her.

Working from home has been my normal for many years, but that normal included a great deal of travel to family and friends and particularly travelling with work. Tony and I often add a holiday on to the end of any work trip abroad and in the UK we normally travel to lectures, arts events, theatre and comedy and music performances all around the country. Of course, all of this has stopped again in the second lockdown as we write in November 2020; almost all of the many venues and events we would have been at have been on hold since March 2020.

One of the other things I do that connects me to the local community and more directly to my beloved arts practice is to help run a community choir for elderly and more recently retired people which has attracted a diverse group of people (living in quite a monocultural area) who are drawn to an extraordinary young leader, originally from South Africa. My role in this group is as participant teaching assistant/events manager. My mum is a member too – her failing memory was one of the drivers of the initiative. I have learnt so much about how very elderly people are still so outgoing and sociable, often seeking something interesting to go to locally, even if their energy, mobility or memory are limiting we all thrive on an hour which is out of our normal and brings the world into real perspective.

Delmer Tzib

I am a history teacher in a high school in Belize. I studied history at the University of Belize and then spent two years in the South Pacific studying for my Masters. History teaching in Belize is fascinating as I teach African history, Mayan history and Caribbean history, all of which make up the history of Belize. This gives you a good idea about the history of the region. I teach 16 to 17-year-old students and this gives me a lot of meat for discussions. It also gives me the opportunity to encourage and develop debate. In the classroom I like taking an analytical and ideological look at society from the point of view of the interconnections between people.

Belize has a very different history to other places in the region. We are part of the Caribbean and part of Central America. We are seen, and see and describe ourselves, as the Caribbean, but we are also Central American. Sometimes we do not look at the historical reasons that we are different from other Caribbean countries.

Louise Whyte

I am a secondary science teacher, teaching biology and chemistry at a British school in Valencia, Spain. It is a private school that teaches the

British curriculum alongside the Spanish subject requirements, so students have a busy timetable. A year before the pandemic the ownership of the school changed hands, so we were already experiencing quite rapid growth and development.

I have been teaching for ten years, three in the UK and seven in Spain. Previously I have held departmental or curriculum responsibilities, but in the September before the Covid-19 pandemic I chose to move schools to return to a full-time teaching role in order to re-focus on my teaching as I feel that secondary education is about to undergo a big change.

At the start of the pandemic, Spain went into a strict lockdown. There was a lack of warning, which meant many students and staff started unprepared. My term finished on Friday as normal and most students took home only their books for the homework that they had been set for the short holiday. We were told to expect up to two weeks off school. But obviously that all changed!

The lockdown in Spain was quite severely restrictive and even though my students are privately educated they did not all have access to good technology for their schoolwork (many had to use their phones as siblings were being taught at the same time), so we lost effective communication with some of them and were concerned for the well-being of many. Children were not allowed to leave the house for six weeks and many of my students live in city apartments with no outside space.

Vicky Van Wyk

I have been living in South East Asia for seven years and was teaching in Myanmar for six years, and I have recently relocated to Thailand. Most of my teaching experience has been in Early Years and Lower Primary settings, where I was previously a homeroom teacher for students between the ages of five to seven years in Yangon. I would teach all subjects except the Native language. Having recently relocated to Bangkok, I moved to an Early Years Foundation Stage (EYFS) setting, and currently teaching 27 three-year-olds. As you can imagine, this is a very different environment for me, as I am used to older students and less than 20 students in one classroom.

I have always been passionate and driven about teaching. I have found it to be a very rewarding career and find immense joy in teaching children the ways of the world and the necessities of life.

Added to my PGCEi, I also hold a Post Graduate Diploma in Play Therapy which I completed through Play Therapy International. I started with the course whilst I was teaching in Myanmar, as I realised many of the students I came across at school with behavioural difficulties had very little support to stimulate their feelings and difficulties at school or at home. It took me four years to complete the course, which was incredibly rewarding. Children with difficulties need someone to facilitate and help them work through their feelings, through means of play, as they are unable to cognitively fully express their emotional well-being as adults can. Often as adults or parents, we too forget to play. We become too serious in our daily lives and might even become too distracted to encourage play at home or school.

In my opinion, Play Therapy is incredibly important for children dealing with any kind of trauma or difficulty. It was essential for me to acquire all the necessary equipment for a playroom, to be able to stimulate any given form of play the child would like to interact with when they are in a session. I was trained to facilitate the play and guide children through their conversations or role play, making use of the knowledge learnt to assess the particular wording or form of play. Conversations with the child would be non-directive, encouraging and allowing them to share their thoughts and feelings in a strictly confidential setting. This allowed children the safety of talking through any forms of difficulty they may have. I soon realised how my in-depth knowledge of Play Therapy has also altered and improved my teaching skills in a classroom; how to better interact with students mindfully, do more check-ins and to listen to the conversations taking place during play time or role play.

Reflections

The educational contexts that we find ourselves in are the result of many journeys and it can be interesting to wonder why we find ourselves in the places that we do. What is it about Tony's educational journey that means he now finds himself in a shed in a Yorkshire town, writing mathematics materials used in international schools around the world? How are Vicky and Edward's journeys similar, as they will be in some ways as they both now teach young children in Bangkok – what differs about their beliefs and values? As we read the descriptions of our current contexts we explored what it was that tied this group of collaborators together.

Unsurprisingly several of the group have worked in a range of countries. Whilst Michael has not taught internationally, the mathematics games that he has placed on his *YouTube* channel have brought him to an international audience. Working internationally has at least two facets. Firstly, it means that we realise we cannot impose a single way of working on all teachers and learners in every country. Different contexts demand different approaches. We can also understand that teachers and learners all around the world face similar challenges. It has been fascinating how teachers have collaborated around the world to work at the challenge of education under the pandemic. Secondly, I think we are more sceptical when we are told that a particular country has 'the answer' for other countries. Because the writers have worked in different settings, they understand that there is no such thing as a single simple solution to an educational problem.

There are several examples of the boundaries between the professional lives and the personal lives of the writers becoming blurred. Tony mentions how supporting his grandchildren's learning of mathematics has developed his understanding of how children learn; Helen sees her roles as carer for her parents as overlapping with her teaching; Michael works with his son on developing his mathematics games and Jasmine's work takes place in family homes. Perhaps this familial feel is something that the group have in common.

Several of the group also seem comfortable moving between roles and taking on new challenges. Vicky and Edward have recently moved to new schools or new roles; Michael has moved out of schools altogether and Amanda teaches in two different settings. In fact, just as the book was being finalised Amanda moved from Brazil to Austria. This movement between roles and settings may mean that these members of the team have developed experience in dealing with new challenges. This movement between settings needs to be balanced by contributors such as Jess and Lucy who, whilst taking on new challenges, have spent considerable time in a single institution.

These short introductions would suggest that the authors are looking for possibilities in the current situation. We realise that we are learning new ways of working very quickly and that we can draw on this learning to inform our practices in the future. These possibilities include new ways of collaboration. Of course, this book is itself a new collaboration that has grown out of the pandemic. I think we are all interested in exploring how such international collaboration can be drawn on to support the learners we work with in the future. As well as this virtual international community, many of the authors work in international settings. Their teaching colleagues come from many different countries; the children that they teach are from global backgrounds, many will be third culture kids. That is, their parents may well have backgrounds in different cultures and the child is being brought up in a third culture.

We also noticed commitment from many of the group of further study. Vicky mentioned her study of Play Therapy; Jasmine is undertaking further study in her field and Mr Muhati, Betty and Louise are all currently studying for the PGCEi at the University of Nottingham. Learning is seen as a lifelong experience and something that can enrich our lives as well as the experiences of those we teach.

Finally, there is a commitment to education for and as social change. Perhaps that is what drew us together more than anything. Jess and Michael talk about how the school they both worked in has a 'socially conscious' approach; Jasmine works with young learners to ensure the challenges they face do not impact on their life chances; Hubert Mweli is working at a national level to ensure the pandemic does not impact learners' life changes adversely and Delmer and Mr Muhati both want to use the teaching of history to explore the connections between people and make sure that Black lives really do matter. Helen suggests a community choir can learn so much about the world and diversity even at a very local level. Finally, Seb raises an important issue for the relationship between the state and the private sector which exists, to differing extents, in all the countries represented by this author team. He notices that the international school sector is much more progressive than the government-controlled sector.

As you read these introductions, you will have found some of the settings familiar and some strange. It has been said that good research 'makes the familiar' strange. It is this making the familiar strange that helps us notice what we take for granted in our own practice. And it is this noticing which allows us to develop and grow as teachers. Now you have met the team. We hope you enjoy reading about their journeys through the pandemic in more detail.

Which of the contributors do you feel an affinity with? Why do you think this is?

Part 2

Responding to the pandemic

Chapter 4

How the setting changed as a result of the pandemic

Introduction

The first thing we asked our co-authors to describe was a typical day in their setting before the pandemic and then to explain the changes that happened both within the setting and in terms of the curriculum when schools entered lockdown. The first thing we realised, of course, is that there is no such thing as a typical day. And that, as soon as schools and educational settings were closed this became unimportant. The focus was directly on how to deal with the day-to-day under lockdown.

It also became clear that the immediate changes did not last. There was an initial response by each school, and by each administration, depending on the country. But, as you will read below, this initial change was often followed by a range of new developments as teachers and administrators learned the benefits and limitations of the new technologies they were working with, very quickly.

Lucy Cooker

The personal and professional impact of the pandemic has been massive for me; it has completely changed my life. As I wrote in the previous chapter, just before the pandemic hit the UK my elderly parents moved to my town, a move that had been planned for some time. Of course, one result of Covid-19 is that I feel much more responsible for their care than I had expected.

Professionally the pandemic has turned my life upside down. Travelling used to be such a large part of my job. I loved my job because of the travel involved. Travelling has always been something that I have loved and has been very much part of who I am and how I construct my identity. This part of my identity has been stripped away overnight.

DOI: 10.4324/9781003150596-4

The first thing I had to deal with was the induction process for the PGCEi course. This has moved from a two-day or a four-day, face-to-face experience to being entirely online. That has been a lot of work and really was a big worry at the time. Implementing this change was really stressful and that, combined with the removal of the joys of travel, has been really difficult. I have worked abroad much of the time; I take holidays abroad and all my research was outside the UK, so losing all of this has not been easy at all. When I think about the last year; mum and dad moving here at the end of June; moving the PGCEi course entirely online for the next two years; taking on my new role in the university, *everything* has changed. I can honestly say my life, in fundamental ways, is unrecognisable to what it was, although, I suppose, the basics are still there.

And yet, you know, I have to keep reminding myself that in the scheme of things those changes have not been so terrible. I really enjoy my new role at the university.

Tony Cotton

I used to go to London once a week or once a fortnight for meetings and I have not been able to do that, but I have not missed that in the slightest. I have actually got a lot more done because I am not wasting time on buses or trains or in meetings that I don't really need. When you do have to be in meetings online, you can sit and do something else when you have your video turned off. In some ways it is a lot more difficult to be engaged and present with a two-dimensional experience than a three-dimensional one.

At the time of this interview, early November 2020, we have recently been moved back into what is called 'Tier 3' here in England where there are a lot of restrictions on daily life. Restaurants, cafes and bars are closed and we are prohibited from meeting many people. However, uncertainty is worse, for example, when the media reports that the government is going to change policy, but then the actual announcement of the detail of that policy takes a few days. Now I know I have just got to sit in my shed for another month and get on with life.

Having said all that, because I mainly worked at home anyway, my day-to-day experience of work has not changed that much. Certainly not as much as for others who were suddenly thrown back at home. We have not really got any distractions here, and if there are distractions I can just come outside and get away from the disturbance. So, in some ways, it has actually been quite nice.

In terms of my day-to-day experiences with education, I normally deliver various live workshops for publishers and other organisations. Obviously, I have not run any of those in-person, but I have delivered several online. That was quite strange. However, I am a big music fan and I have learned about online interactions from friends and other people doing gigs online. For example, before the gig, they might have a discussion with the audience, saying 'hi' and just acknowledging who is in the room. I learned from this and have built it into all of my online training. I have also tried to get to know a little about the participants' individual experience by drawing on what they have been doing in the country in which they live and work. When I ran an online workshop for primary mathematics teachers in Belize, I got them to send me photographs of shapes outside their window. Or as part of the activities they would talk about how big the room they were sitting in was. In some ways it is very powerful to sit here in my shed in Otley and there is somebody in Moscow and somebody in Mongolia and somebody in Thailand and somebody in Korea all just sitting in the same screen. But I still find it hard to really get a handle on what people are actually thinking and understanding. Not having that instant feedback you get from a 'live' group is quite difficult. I have never been somebody who educates by telling, just reading through a slide presentation. 'Normally', I will have a few slides, but I am never quite sure what direction the presentation will go in. I tend to see what is particularly interesting or inspiring to a particular group and go in that direction. You cannot really have that same spontaneity when you are working online. I cannot improvise or develop ideas as much. I get the sense that learning is going on on the other side of my computer screen but in ways which are informal rather than intense listening or doing when I am working with people in the same room as me.

Edward Emmet

We have been open almost as normal for a long time. We were teaching wearing masks for two months before the pandemic hit because Bangkok had really bad pollution, but with air filters in the classroom we always take them off. I think Asian culture is one which is much more used to wearing masks than Europeans.

Halfway through a normal teaching week we closed overnight on the government's decision. There was an immediate scramble to produce all materials for all lessons online. Everything went online, but we did not have any systems in place to facilitate this really. We do use *Class Dojo*, so we have communication with parents and they immediately used this to demand lessons for their children; our fees are quite high and they felt the pressure with their children at home.

We worked from home for one week. I arranged to go into the music room to record drum tracks for songs for the children to learn, but everything else was produced at home and I ordered any resources I needed and paid for them myself as everything is so cheap in Thailand. Every subject had to be taught online. Lessons were written and recorded by our team of three teachers which were then posted on 'chats' for the first week. The school then gave us three weeks 'off' to set up Google classrooms. Previously, we did have meetings and share ideas, but we had never worked together in such a co-ordinated way; when this happened we had to decide exactly what we were doing and share our lessons.

We fairly quickly realised that we could not replicate the whole school day online, so the timetable was not a full schedule after this three weeks planning. The structure of the day was from 9 am English, then Mathematics, followed by theme or topic work. Not every lesson was live. Every day we had a feedback session with our class at the end of the day between 4 and 4.30 pm. We chose some lessons to be live and others were recorded. Some lessons were not feasible to teach live. I think on average it was about 50/50.

At first, we were not allowed in school at all for safety reasons which felt very odd as our campus pre-Covid was a very busy place. Later you had to book a time to go to school to collect anything you needed. The school grounds are big and were cordoned off to keep staff and site staff safe. I brought white boards and a drum kit home and my spare room became a classroom. Classroom assistants were in constant touch, but mostly I didn't ask them to do much as I ordered equipment online.

Jessica Greenbaum

Everything has changed. At first it felt like the social experience of education had been taken away completely. Schools being closed meant there was a lack of opportunity to be social. Remote teaching became purely academic. The tasks were very curriculum based, mainly around literacy and numeracy focus with little opportunity for rich discussion. There were not the usual class meetings between teachers and students which I would have when we were in school to discuss what had been going on in the classroom.

Over time have I learned how to build in the social. For example, we have a class meeting every morning on the platform we use for remote teaching. I open the meeting 15 minutes early and all the classes are invited. For the first five minutes I turn my microphone and video off and the children have free talking. Only after this do we all talk about the task. I have 27 in my class in total, maybe half come in for that social interaction. Often only four do the talking, but the others listen. I think this listening is really important too. I do not understand quite a lot of what is going on, but it is hilarious. It feels like these are the kids who rock up to school early and really enjoy and value informal time together before school. It has been great to be able to provide this space virtually.

Something else that is different is the lack of flexibility in planning and teaching. As everything is planned in advance I cannot be as flexible. I cannot change things on the hoof like I used to do if I did not feel like I was meeting the student's needs.

Jasmine Irani

There were two stages to the changes that happened, both within school and in terms of the curriculum, when the schools entered lockdown. In March the change was sudden. We only heard about things happening the week before. Even the week before school closed a family who I had been working in-home with self-isolated, stopping sessions; they had no symptoms, but their child has a weakened immune system, so they took extra precautions.

In some cases, it was appropriate to move to one-to-one *Zoom* sessions where we were able to work on a mixture of both academic and social targets. These targets varied from case to case; for example, with a six-year-old in a mainstream setting, we looked at writing skills. He was quite reluctant to write, so we would work on fun mark-making activities to increase his confidence and familiarity, like pen races and doodling. Or, we might start with drawing games and then move onto letter formation, linking this to tasks he preferred, such as labelling his drawings or writing secret messages. Another target might be to copy letters with the correct letter formation or to develop conversation skills (particularly keeping conversations going, for example, responding to a question and then asking a follow-up question. We also worked on emotional regulation, that is, identifying how you are feeling; identifying strategies you can use if you are feeling worried or anxious and practising them.

In contrast with a three-year-old early learner, we were talking parents through working on targets. These were things like play targets which might be playing alongside their child (parallel play) to encourage their child to watch and engage in the play. Or early communication targets such as using physical behaviours like reaching, imitating, moving or handling objects to continue a sensory social routine.

All our groups moved online for no more than two hours a week. In terms of targets for group sessions – we would have a skill of the week. Examples are 'stinky thinking' (which of your thoughts are negative 'brain farts', noticing them, the differences between facts and opinions and what positive thoughts about ourselves can we have); 'cool conversations' (how to keep a conversation going, how to tell if someone's interested in what you're saying, how to choose topics of conversation); 'super-flex' (how can we be super flexible, in our thoughts and in our actions? The opposite of super flex is a 'rock brain!', what cool things might happen if we are super flexible and go with the flow, what things can we do and try to be super flexible).

Mondays we would email out the 'Skill of the Week' and a selection of corresponding activities, conversation and drawing challenges, craft activities, games to play with their families and things to prepare for the Friday *Zoom*, such as jokes and good news to share. The vague structure of the face-to-face sessions was kept in place for the *Zoom* session. We would go over the rules, play favourite games, do learning activities and generally get to know and trust each other and so on. What changed was that it was really lovely getting to know one another over *Zoom*. We tried to be playful online, so we would 'joke share' or play favourite games from the face-to-face sessions over *Zoom* like 'fish and chips' or 'natural disasters'. Joke share, learning a joke every week to share with the group, became very popular. The 'detectives' became more creative, and wild, as the weeks went on. Fabulous in-jokes began to develop as the group got to know each other better and a 'good news share!' telling everyone about something good that had happened during the week, practising focusing on the good in dark times, an important skill for all of us!

Sessions would have between four and eight 'Detectives' (children) attend. There would usually be three to four Lieutenants (staff) – those with less experience with the children might run just one activity in the *Zoom session*, another person might be with them to record data such as where there had been 'reciprocal conversations', or other specific targets that had been identified for the Detective to work on.

Seb Jefferies

We went online very successfully; in fact, we have gained students through the success of the online programme. Going online was certainly a busy time, but it was eased by good communication and a competent and understanding IT department. To start with, for the first few weeks we uploaded worksheets, but after that things became far more interactive as students and teachers became more comfortable with different online learning platforms.

We have since had to go online again due to a community outbreak; while this is unfortunate, we have been able to learn from the last time we went online. This time around we are providing more online classes in real time rather than recorded lessons. I have found this to be far better for student outcomes and it has also given us more chances to check in on students and their social and emotional well-being. This lockdown has been rather strict, but online lessons have provided a much-needed slice of near normality to the working day. My students, as ever, have been cheerful, mostly diligent, and proved that they can adapt most wonderfully to change.

Even though we were distant from the students we made the lessons interactive. We set a task or sent a video of ourselves carrying out an activity and the students would upload a video of themselves doing the task which I could look at. It was really impressive how the parents and other siblings got involved in the tasks too.

It is a big thing in Mongolia that elder siblings help out. It's sort of expected that they will do a bit of parenting. It is also pretty usual that one of the parents will be at home. This is not always the mum; there are lots of very successful women who are CEOs of companies, so the dad is the one at home with the children.

Michael Minas

Prior to the pandemic nearly all my work had been in schools – running professional development sessions for staff; teaching model lessons for teachers; working alongside teachers in a range of ways. When the schools closed, a lot of my work stopped and so I had to come up with alternatives, very quickly.

I had more time on my hands, so I thought through what would be helpful to the schools that I had been working with. The genesis really came when I saw a family I know setting up for a mathematics lesson at home. They were sitting with their child with a mathematics textbook in front of them ready to start 'work'. I thought we must be able to come up with something better than that.

I have always had this belief that if you think the parents are on the wrong track, we need to ask whose responsibility is that? I think part of our job is to bring the parents along with us. So, I decided to post mathematics games online, to show parents what they could be doing as an alternative to working through a textbook. It has been interesting because lots of kids in the schools I have been working in have contacted me to say they love the games.

Amanda Queiroz Moura

The changes were different depending on the education sector and on the social situation of the students. In the private college I work in, teaching engineers, we had socially distanced lessons on the Monday, then from the Tuesday we were online. For all the online teaching they have the necessary equipment and IT support. It is a crazy system at the moment; the college has not given me any holidays at all during the pandemic. Teaching algebra to these engineering students is really challenging and responding to the mathematics online is a difficulty for them as it is hard to 'write' mathematics using a normal computer keyboard.

The assessments mean they have to respond to some quite complex questions. As a way of solving this problem we give students the option to upload a picture of their written work. This was my experience for the last semester. Now the students are very tired. At first, they were scared of the pandemic, no one relaxed. I never had a break. At the college, the online time was around two hours. However, teenagers from private high school have around six hours of online classes every day. They were very tired by it all.

I have friends who teach in the Brazilian public school sector. These teachers were given the usual holiday break to create online delivery systems for lessons using online platforms or TV channels to deliver the content. They then shared classes to all students, but some do not have IT at home and so could not access the lessons. Telephone connections were supposed to be available in all areas so that students could access *YouTube* channels for learning. What actually happened? Some students do not even have a notebook, no self-funds, so, perhaps, only one child in a family can be educated. Parents were working during class time and so could not support their children. Some families did not have the signal from the phone company because the networks do not go that far out. If a neighbour had a signal too many children would ask to use it at once. They then shared classes with all students, but some do not have internet or a computer at home and so could not access the lessons. Some students tried to access the system using cell phones, but telephone connections were supposed to be available in all areas so that students could access channels for learning, which not was possible.

WhatsApp is very popular in Brazil, we use it for lots of purposes. Teachers tried to use *WhatsApp* to send activities to all their students, even it was a mess because the students did not respect the time of the classes. *WhatsApp* was the more efficient way to communicate with the students and parents. Some schools printed activities out and asked students to go to their school and pick them up. Not many students went to their schools to collect the activities.

I went to live with my parents in a city near Sao Paulo and stayed with them for three months. but I continued teaching classes online. However, the school ordered holidays during the month of April to allow us to plan for and organise online classes. Now I live with two friends; we invent 'happy hours' play games, a lot of creative things. Watch a movie and comment on it. I also did some research talks for teacher training in critical mathematics education from home. We don't imagine enough how to use our research in the classroom. I give a lot of talks about my research every week. Online meetings of the research group used raising hands to speak but now we use the chat boxes.

Nicodemus Amboko Muhati

The pandemic has transformed everything. Things have changed left, right and centre now as a classroom practitioner. Let me talk about two things, first the experience of the students in the learning environment and second the support that you get and give to and from colleagues.

Before the outbreak of this pandemic, I was used to engaging my students within the four walls of a classroom. As a teacher of history, I love using a wide range of methods when delivering the content. Mostly in my teaching, I employ student-centred pedagogy. However, when schools closed and we started remote teaching and learning, you cannot engage your students one on one and students cannot easily form groups and engage each other. Engaging my students online has come with a lot of challenges. For example, if I'm teaching about Hitler and I want to ask a student to act as a journalist reporting on Germany engaging another country in war, it is difficult because most of my students like the 'kinesthetic' aspects of learning. They move around and I use their energy in the classroom. Now students can be found just seated behind the screen and they tell you at the beginning that the lesson is boring. We cannot do any drama. You cannot run from the corner of the class to this at the end of the class. So, I found I was using a limited number of teaching methods most of the time. The problem with solely verbal communication is that not every student in my class will want to talk. Some will want to draw, some will want to dramatise. So, the main challenge with remote teaching and learning is that it has limited me in terms of knowing how far I can go with my students.

At the beginning of the pandemic, we used *Zoom* for teaching, but then it was found not to be safe for children online because sometimes you are teaching and then you find a stranger in class and you cannot really tell whether they are a student so it was not very safe. So, my school decided that we were going to do away with *Zoom* completely. Now the policy is very clear. It is only the *Google Meet* now because in *Google Meet* we have *Google Classroom* which has been configured with the school account. You generate the link from the *Google Classroom* and share that with students so the access is restricted. The school will be able to access your classroom. And a parent can request access. In that case arrangements will be made beforehand and the link will be activated for them. They will be able to join the class. Sometimes that is for the first ten minutes or the first 20 minutes just to see what is happening and the kids will be informed in advance so that they know.

In terms of support given to and given by colleagues, it used to be that I could walk into the next office and engage my colleagues and ask them questions. We would be experiencing these challenges together and we would be able to think together and come up with possible remedies, or know how can we make teaching and learning enjoyable for our students.

Betty Sheila Mumbi

The first case of Covid-19 was reported on a Friday. Some colleagues of mine and I were actually on our way to Nairobi for a hockey tournament the following Saturday and we got a call from school to turn back and come home. We did not know what was happening. When we got back we were briefed and we were told there had been a reported case of Covid-19 and the government had put a stop to all sporting events. We were unable to attend any tournaments or host any schools, so we cancelled all those events. This happened on a Friday and on the Sunday we were told that all schools needed to shut down by the following Wednesday. We literally had two or three days to prepare for our school to close. It was quite a difficult shift as all the schools closed at once all across the country.

There has also been quite a shift in my day-to-day experiences because teaching PE usually means I am out on the field most of the time. Now with online learning I am sitting in one place throughout the day, taking occasional breaks, going outside for a walk, and then back on the screen again. I have never had this much screen time in my life, ever. I do try to manage my day carefully according to when I am on screen and when I am off screen. I ensure that I have at least two hours to myself. I can go out and run or go for a swim, or take a walk just to get off the screen.

Trying to create content for PE in the first three weeks after the school closed was quite a task because we did not know whether kids have space in their houses or not and we didn't know whether they have appropriate equipment or not. So, it was quite a difficult task, as opposed to in school, where I know exactly the conditions within which I am working and the number of kids attending at any one time. Some of the major challenges in learning have included a loss in the physical connection with students. As you can imagine, teaching PE online is not easy as you have limited control over what every student is doing and so giving feedback and monitoring work has not been easy.

At first, it was pretty much just trying to get them to continue with the skills we were learning. I remember when we closed the school we were focusing on hockey. We were due to attend the last hockey tournament before moving on to rugby and netball and the plan was to keep students engaged and learning both skills. But after deliberation and feedback from students and parents, we decided to focus on fitness, just making sure the kids are not on the screen the entire time. We have a time for fitness and a session for skills. They learn athletic skills, ball skills at least once a week. They do get to learn some sort of skills and then we also set out some cross-curricular themes for them too. There was also some negotiation with individuals. We allowed them to be active in any way they decided to. Whether they could go running or whether they were able to go swimming, as long as they can evidence the activity and then send it back to us, we can then see how far they are going with the skill. For example, if they run, we gave them options of different *apps* they can use. We found a sports training app and an app for training auditors that were both easy to use. They shared these records with us, and when they shared them, it showed exactly what they did, and on what date. If they're swimming, they can take tell us how far they swam and how long it took. They can have someone video them. If it is football then they can take a video and then share it on *Teams* so we can see how they have progressed over the weeks.

When we started, in the first few weeks, we did not use video for quite a while, because of safeguarding issues and because we were not sure how it would go with some students. This meant we could not see students and they could not see us, which was quite a barrier for communication. This also made enforcing discipline in lessons an uphill task. But as we have grown with it then we have been able to see kids and the kids have been able to see us. It has been a really great growth process. So now we do video calls with them every morning. Every morning of the week we sit together. We pray together; we talk about their day the previous day; what they hope to do in the day. It is really interesting.

In terms of teaching Humanities, the only thing that has really changed between online and physical teaching is just the notebooks. Because it's pretty much the same content that we are doing that we would have covered in class. The only difference is that now most of the students have to do research online or on websites that we provide as opposed to the textbooks we would use if we were in school. Everything else has pretty much been the same as the physical set-up. We are talking to our students, but instead of talking to them from the front or the side of the classroom, we are talking to them through *Teams*. I think *Microsoft Teams* is very efficient when it comes to sharing schoolwork. All I need to do is plan my lesson in my notebook and then share it with students in all their different notebooks. When they complete it then I just have to go into the students' notebooks to mark it.

Virtual learning has been a great learning experience, and also a challenging one. Adapting to using this much technology for education has been such an experience. Lesson planning and implementation, as well as feedback to ensure learning is taking place, has been great. Lesson differentiation for online learning has been an area of major focus, as well as making the lessons interactive and captivating for students.

One of the main things that teaching virtually has taught me at this time is the need to keep a connection with students. This way, regardless of distance and circumstances, they can always reach out to me if they are experiencing difficulties with lessons, or experiencing pastoral issues, or even dealing with cyber bullying. Maintaining a safe space for students has been key.

Hubert Mathanzima Mweli

We have had to give priority to the health and safety protocols for Covid-19. Initially, educators, learners and communities expressed concern and, in some instances, anxiety and fear to return to work and school. I think that confidence in the system has grown as schools demonstrate the ability to maintain the safety standards and as infections in students and staff have continued to decline. For example, there has been little resistance to the use of masks in schools at all times which was instructed by the Department of Basic Education. We have the data to show that the re-opening of schools has not affected community transmission. In fact, our attendance rates are amongst the highest seen in countries that have re-opened across the world. This is something we are really proud of.

There are still many challenges such as finding the space and the educator numbers to maintain the necessary physical distancing and a lack of additional funding for the procurement of Covid-19 essentials. This has meant taking resources away from core education priorities and plans to ensure the Covid-19 priorities are met. Schools have responded to these challenges with innovations such as markings in classrooms and corridors to ensure social distancing.

Helen Toft

In terms of my day-to-day working the pandemic appeared to change very little. Apart from the one weekend of face-to-face sessions each year all my teaching and support of students is online anyway as the PGCEi students are spread all around the world. The biggest change was cancelling the weekly older people's choir from an 'in person' session. Thanda and I did not know how we were going to organise this successfully.

Lockdown hit me very hard. The huge responsibility for my mum, the choir members and many vulnerable older people in my town. Issues with it being safe to continue caring for our grandchildren in a town to which we normally travelled once a week. What if I spread the virus to the vulnerable people I was caring for? This anxiety meant I could not engage with anything but my own day-to-day organisation; I was very anxious about keeping those I care for safe.

Fortunately, this was a shared response. My students on the PGCEi course were going through lockdowns at a similar time and they were experiencing all sorts of anxieties. They were being shut out of schools in which they taught and studied for the PGCEi with less than 24 hours' notice, which reinforced my understanding of the extent of the impact of the pandemic around the world. This had been so slow to dawn on me and to understand the enormity and complexity. I made sure that I kept in close contact with all my students to check in on them to make sure they were okay. I found that contact moving, intense and important; the students' perspectives, some had already gone through it and come out on the other side, were very encouraging and they were saying, 'this virus can be controlled and online teaching can be made to work'.

I had been dreading online teaching because of the lack of the face-to-face element – looking into each other's eyes. But they gave me the confidence to give it a go, to support my elderly choir members more confidently at their doors if they could not make the online sessions Thanda began for those who could access them. It was an intensely emotional time, and it shook me just how much time it took me to build enough resilience to deal with it.

Delmer Tzib

By the end of March we knew that the virus and a shutdown of schools was coming. So when it hit I thought, 'Okay, how is this going to work'? When the announcement came that schools would close, teachers, or departments actually, were tasked to come up with academic continuity plans (ACPs). We had to suggest how we would move forward, and the school proposed *Google classroom* as the platform for interacting with students. We all signed up for that. Now there was a new term in our vocabulary, 'asynchronous learning'. This became part of the language about how we would teach moving forward, posting information for our classes, posting instructions online for our students to follow. At this stage the online lessons were following exactly the same timetable as when the students were at school, but we did not know when the students were logging on to engage with the material. This was the first reaction to the relatively unplanned shutdown of schools and the nation.

By the third day of school closure, we realised that this was not working. There was simply too much material online and it was the students that were suffering. It was also an incredible burden on the teachers. Many of them were simply not submitting, so we changed the schedule to offering 15-minute snippets of stimulus for each lesson. This seemed to be a more student-focused approach.

I had planned for a structured online classroom, a structured session for the students. The key elements of this structure were:

- Clear aims for the learning so the students knew what I hoped they would learn from their engagement with the materials
- Links to other units so they knew where the learning fit with other units of study
- An overview of the process that they would be following
- A set of instructions, 'watch this video', 'read this set of readings'
- A graphic organiser
- A slide presentation which pulled all the material together

In addition to this there was an analytical assignment each week. This was not based on asking students to recall facts. I might ask them to create a cartoon that explained or critiqued a situation we had been studying; I might ask them to analyse newspapers. I hoped I was assessing their analytical and critical skills.

That is how the first two weeks went. The amount of planning for the online teaching was huge. After those two weeks we were already at Easter and we had a break. As we got towards Easter it had seemed as though the students were affected by the growth of cases of the virus in the country and were becoming worried. Again, the engagement rates with the online platforms had gone down. After Easter, I started to use other tools so that I could appear online, I could actually become a presence in the classroom even though the learning was still non-synchronous. I recorded myself teaching and embedded these videos in the slide presentations. When the students could actually see me, the engagement increased. They could still access the slide presentations whenever they wanted. Even though there was no sense of the teaching being live, it did help them build that direct contact that they are used to in school. I think this was about how could I keep the students' attention using the internet or the computer and how do I, as a teacher, remain a calm and calming presence for the students throughout the process.

When the government of Belize decided to re-open schools in September 2020, the approaches and strategies had changed. The faculty was called to school to attend meetings and see our way forward. It was decided that we would go fully online and that students would experience six classes online for 50 minutes each and breaks in between. We were given lighter loads as teachers to prepare for our classes. We were required to be live for our students to see us and interact with us. This process at first was strenuous because of internet issues. Many students struggled and are still struggling to get a good device or get quality access to the internet.

However, our school created a plan for assistance to the teachers and also to the students. The school hired a consultant to help us through and I think so far we are coping well with the experience. There are still some minor issues, but it is an ongoing process of change.

Louise Whyte

My day-to-day experiences have changed dramatically throughout the last year. Initially, we had remote learning, then teaching online, followed by a phased return for older students before the summer holiday. Since September all classes were back in school but with a range of strict restrictions and all of these experiences were very distinctly different from a normal school year. When we were online, students were at home and out of their normal routine with a variety of access to resources. The first couple of weeks were tough and I met with colleagues to determine what we could implement to ensure students were engaging in learning. The main outcome was to reduce the number of learning objectives and activities each lesson to make sure that students could achieve according to their level; make sure they were quite happy with that one aspect by giving clear feedback before moving on. Online, we found that the students were differentiating for themselves quite successfully and they were becoming more independent. They persevered with a task before submitting it. Now we're back in the classroom, they've lost that a little bit.

The media and our interactions with them has also had an influence. They have heard in the news that they have missed a lot of school and how that could put them behind. We keep asking them if they are OK, a lot more than we would do normally. The children seem to be becoming quite worried and lost about a lot of things. We need to provide more reassurance and structure than maybe we would have done before. Some of the students' English speaking and comprehension skills have dropped quite a lot as well, so I think there is a little bit of hesitancy with some of the students about that.

The social distancing rules mean that we cannot move around the classroom as much as before. So previously I might have come up and prompted someone. Now it is not so easy to do that and it seems that the students are less able to work through problems for themselves than before the pandemic or when working online.

The students have never had such a big change. The majority have been in the same class in the same school since they were three. This is such a big upheaval for so many of them. Everything is so different, break times and learning areas are different; socialising is difficult; activities and lessons are very different. Students and teachers wear masks at all times. I think the changes we are seeing with students and their confidence are to do with the continued presence of Covid-19 in their daily lives.

Vicky Van Wyk

We were only notified the day prior that schools would shut down. There was very little information in the news, so unfortunately, there was no time to talk to the students on what may happen or how the situation would progress. All the schools in Yangon shut and my particular school did not open, even online, for two months. Everyone was trying to come to an understanding of what was happening and what we should worry about. At that stage there were only a few odd Covid-19 cases in Myanmar. When online learning finally opened up, very few students joined in. There are still many technical issues with regards to service for wi-fi in many parts of Myanmar, as well as many power cuts, so it became almost impossible for some families to join classes with limited resources and connection.

Most teachers left the country while the borders were still open and returned home. There was a big concern for friends and families, rightly so, and at that moment in time, teaching may not have been a top priority for everyone. This meant that some parents and children were becoming anxious about the situation at hand. Unfortunately, many young children struggle with expressing this anxiety. Parents were not used to being at home with their children. I remember one phone call I had from an anxious mother, looking for advice on how to calm her little one down, as it seemed she was having difficulty with this. It was humbling but very sad too. It shows that there is a huge gap in parenting skills with some families. This particular struggle on how to interact with their children was really difficult to deal with online.

The school I worked at was a mid-tier international school, affordable quality education. This meant some families had limited resources for online learning. At first it was very trying for myself and the students. The school's expectation was to replicate the normal school day's experience for children online. So, for the first week I had my class students (well, about ten of them) to teach online. First, I had to teach them to use *Zoom* and whilst I was doing this they were often distracted by their parents. It was quite trying to keep their attention and sitting in front of a screen for a long period of time was hard on their eyes. Unfortunately, there was no sane way to do group work, which I quite enjoyed and made use of in my classroom.

I also noticed that I had to adapt the way I was speaking and conducting lessons, making sure I am heard and listened to over all the background distractions and talking parents. The hard part for me was that I had to remain mindful that the children were having a much more challenging experience than I was. They were not seeing any of their friends and social interaction was minimal. Many of these students lived in apartment blocks with no garden or balconies, making it difficult for them to take a break from the whole day at home.

After the first week, I started doing many more interactive activities. I put the textbook aside, where it became an added extra. I tried to introduce a lot of talking time. We would play games and read books together. I would involve the children much more actively and this would focus them, where they would have fun and enjoy class time. I knew there may be some added pressure at home with parents working remotely as well, so there may be less interaction than what was needed. My thought was that my presence online could be their only opportunity for fun interaction during the day. Keep in mind that these children are supposed to be in kindergarten, they are meant to play, their sensorial skills need to be developed and they should be having fun.

Reflection

The first thing that struck us reading through these accounts was the suddenness of the change. Several authors expressed just this, 'Suddenly everything changed'. Betty had to turn the minibus round on the way to a sporting event. Vicky was told the day before that her school would be closed and she would be teaching online the next day. Some of us found this experience being repeated. In the UK after the Christmas holiday break all children returned to school on the Monday only to be told that evening that schools would be closed the following day. This sudden change limited the amount of planning that was possible and meant that we were all learning very quickly, particularly during the first periods of lockdown. Some countries gave teachers more planning time than others, but there is a sense of the impact that such sudden changes had on everyone, both professionally and personally. Our family and caring routines were suddenly all thrown up in the air too. We also had to negotiate new ways of working and new venues for our workplaces too. And this was easier for some than others. It is, perhaps, easier to teach History and PE remotely. What is inspiring is the ways that we all solved particular problems, often collaboratively, from doorstep visits to the elderly to PE shifting its focus to fitness evidenced using training *apps* to children taking photographs of their mathematical explorations because it is very difficult to use a QWERTY keyboard to write mathematical symbols.

There was some impact on how we perceived ourselves and impacts on our professional identities. We realised that the type of travel we had been engaged in was not going to be a part of our lives for the foreseeable future; that the closeness of team games would disappear, that the sense of community we developed and provided for our learners was going to be hard to sustain. But again, we innovated to find new ways to work. International webinars allowed us to draw educators from all around the world together in ways that are impossible physically. Tony remembers listening to Jess describing how she opened up the chat room early to allow her children to 'socialise' before lessons and building this into his teacher education webinars. Jasmine developed the joke of the week and the good news share to ensure the sense of close community was not lost and Betty describes the joy of 'virtually' meeting her learners every morning.

The tension between school or government expectations to 'deliver' a similar curriculum to the school-based curriculum could be assessed in the same way to the teachers understanding that 'things have to be different' when we are using such a different way of learning and teaching. In Belize online learning and assessment could not lead to your grades being reduced, only getting higher, for example. Michael describes setting up his *YouTube* channel to offer an alternative to simply offering learners 'worksheets'. Tony and Helen quickly had to decide which parts of a two-day online induction needed 'live' elements and which would be best dealt with asynchronously. The main tension seems to be the shift from face-to-face 'lessons' lasting a fixed amount of time before learners move to another subject and lesson. Seb describes how his practice moved to offering brief inputs which children could use as inspiration for individual activity during the day, at a time they chose. These tensions also leave us with questions to work on:

- How can we teach in a student-centred way when we are working online?
- How can we make the best use of teaching assistants working online?
- How do we assess learner understanding when they are learning online?
- How can we develop a community of learners when we are all working in separate spaces?

We wondered what the impact of cultural expectations around learning and teaching had on the way in which we were able to develop online learning. Seb suggests that in Mongolia there is an expectation that siblings will support each other and that parents will expect to support their children in learning. Others report an expectation from parents that the online lessons will 'occupy' their children whilst they attend to their own needs in terms of working from home. It is certain that the types of activity and the content of the curriculum is clearer to parents and carers as a result of home schooling. Maybe one of the biggest challenges or areas we can exploit is how online learning can allow us to develop our relationships with parents and the wider community. More of that later.

Finally, there is a sense that one of the things we found hardest and still struggle with is how we can support learners, and our colleagues, as we all work our way through living under the pandemic. It does feel as though the curriculum, the way that we work, needs to change to acknowledge the very different times we find ourselves in. We cannot just pretend that everything is the same and we are just learning online now. That is not good for the mental health of teachers and learners alike.

Personal reflection on 'How the setting changed as a result of the pandemic'.

What have you learned from your personal experience of teaching and learning under the pandemic?

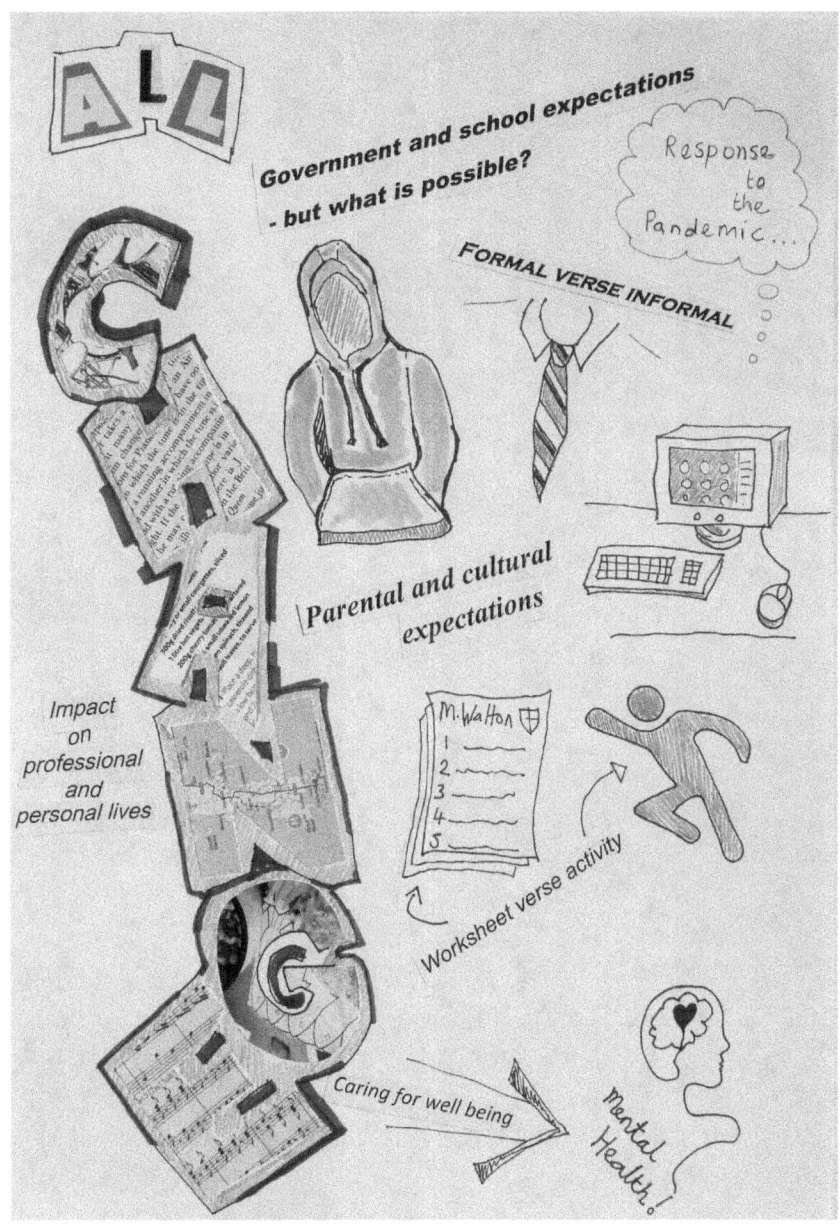

Chapter 5

How relationships with colleagues changed

Introduction

When I work with beginning teachers, I (Tony) often suggest that they deliberately stop doing something that has become habitual. For example, I have banned people from starting a lesson by saying, 'Can you remember what we learned last time'. I once took the teacher's desk away from the front of the classroom and moved it to the back of the classroom to be used as a shared table for group work. I have suggested that teachers tell the students in their classes not to put their hands up after a question has been asked. By removing these habitual practices, we are forced into a position of doing something differently. We have to think of an alternative way to find out what students have remembered from a previous lesson. I was forced to come out from behind my desk and work with students in their preferred spaces. If there are no hands up, offering answers, we have to think carefully about both the questions that we ask and which of the students we will choose to answer.

Another of the things that we might take for granted is the way that we work with our colleagues. Perhaps one of the things that working under the pandemic has done is to make us focus more carefully on the importance of these relationships and how to use and develop these relationships for the benefits of the learners in our care.

Lucy Cooker

My role is static and 'samey' on one level, but on others it has felt rather chaotic. Officially I started my new management role on 1 August but, in reality, it was June. From March I had just been thinking about moving the PGCEi online and keeping the workload down for staff. I felt

DOI: 10.4324/9781003150596-5

the most important thing about my role as a manager and leader was to not create additional worries and anxiety for colleagues as I was seeing how colleagues were responding to all the changes. So, keeping something achievable and relevant for them, to be able to teach on the PGCEi course effectively, was really important to me. Now in my new wider role I try to make colleagues' lives as stress free as possible, but I know it is not going to be easy as some of the systems we have got used to have not been able to adapt quickly to the pressures that teaching and learning under the restrictions have brought. Systems that we used to be able to rely on are no longer operating efficiently and this causes problems. Implementing changes on the other courses they teach on is going to add to their stress because the system is not up to it. Added to this, colleagues who are wedded to the travel part of teaching on the PGCEi have found it really stressful to not be able to do that for the foreseeable future. Losing the opportunity to travel has been hard for them as well as for me.

In terms of wanting to make changes to what we implemented as the lockdown hit, I think there is far too much of my presence in the PGCEi online induction. I did this to avoid putting pressure on other tutors, but this is at the expense of them feeling as though they own the induction. Many colleagues were too busy with changes on other courses, perhaps courses they managed, and everything was very last minute. A key colleague who would have been very good at making video inputs was moved to another role. As courses began in different regions across the world, we were told to use what we had already done, but with our students we could not have used videos that were labelled as Kuala Lumpa in Valencia, or as part of an induction in Bangkok. In order to make sure the inductions happened, I had to create whole cohort videos for the PGCEi early in the morning when my dog would not be barking in the background. It was very early, my hair was long from lockdown and I did not feel as confident as I wanted to be, but at least we have these examples to look back on and improve.

I also had to take part in the welcome week for the whole of the School of Education. We knew we would have up to 500 students present, so we had to use a broadcast form of *Teams* with someone else in control of the slides and my camera. Doing the university welcome for students for the first time as a live event would have been hard but doing it as a broadcast with no feedback from faces in the room was really challenging. With the live *Teams* sessions at least there is the 'chat' or a few have their cameras on initially, so you get a sense of who is there. But with this it was like how it must be reading the news; you know the audience is out there but you cannot see them. That was interesting and involved another whole way of learning to work differently.

Most of my work consists of meetings online and I do not think I need to say anything about that as everyone does this. There are benefits, of course, such as eating your lunch and listening in to a meeting, but there is an intensity to everything being on screen and it becomes very tiring. I think part of this fatigue is about being human and the need to be with each other. Speaking to you now, in this online interview, works really well because we know each other so well, but with people you know less well, you have to work really hard to build a connection and have a real sense of communication.

I do not think being online has affected relationships with colleagues either positively or otherwise. Perhaps it is more difficult to resolve problems rather than having the person in your office. The teaching relationships I have online have been great, both with colleagues who are established on the course and the new team. People are really understanding and supportive of each other.

Tony Cotton

Because of the work that I do and the ways in which I work, I am not sure relationships between key colleagues have changed all that much. I spend all my time with Helen (my wife and co-author) and we have had quite important and useful conversations. As for contacting and meeting with my editors and with publishers, well, they are just keen that I get the job done and you can almost do that more easily and quickly on email rather than any other approach. So I am not sure these relationships have changed all that much. I have not felt isolated from people because the ways that I interact with the people who are important to my working life have not necessarily changed as a result of the shift to remote working.

Perhaps I had already made that shift. I remember when I was Head of the School of Education, I used to pride myself that I would be first in and often the last one to leave. I would make sure the building was welcoming for everyone when they arrived and that I was available if any of my staff needed to see me before they started their day's work. The other thing I always used to do was to look at the emails that had come in overnight and if there were any angry or frustrated emails I would make sure I visited that person's office so we could sort the issue outright at the beginning of the day. It was very much easier to sort these frustrations out face to face rather than online. I suppose not being in that managerial role anymore relieves me of that responsibility.

Edward Emmet

Relationships with colleagues went OK in lockdown. We were experiencing the same stress as each other and supported each other, but nothing in the way we worked together really changed. There was a lot of stress on management to handle issues personally, as we were all having a lot of complaints from parents. They were not prepared for how much work they had to do to support their children and asked why the school had to be closed even though this was a government decision.

Teamwork was challenging as we were not used to it; we had to record and upload every single piece of work for all lessons. For a month we had no free time at all, I was working from six in the morning to 11 at night every day for a month without any break. We were given a pay-cut and everyone was stressed out. There were no major fallings out, though. We just had to focus on changing things if we could not get the technology to work as we wanted, alongside dealing diplomatically with complaints. The amount of work involved to upload, support parents and mark all the work, well, there just were not enough hours of the day. I had no breaks, no free time. In fact, the first four weeks of lockdown was the most stressed I have ever been as a teacher. Perhaps there was no time to develop the relationships with colleagues.

Jessica Greenbaum

I think this has been really interesting. We were moving towards team planning, but a lot of individual practice in our own classrooms had been allowed and had developed over time. So, even though we had planned together some teachers would 'do their own thing'.

Remote learning has wiped that individual practice away. *Google classroom* has meant that we had to work together as what we planned was being shared with all students across the grade level. I see this as a really positive change. We have become much more collaborative and there is a space for a professional challenge. We need to find ways to challenge each other and these are conversations which we were not used to having. All of a sudden, the collaborative planning was directly affecting your kids. So, if I disagreed with something someone was planning, I had to find a way to challenge them. I think this has brought us closer together as a staff.

When we returned to school for three weeks the team planning continued, and we carried on using *Google classroom*. People who are more proficient in a particular area took responsibility for planning that area.

Jasmine Irani

Working the way I do, moving between different households and settings, I realised I was a potential spreader of the virus. We had a *Zoom* partners meeting to discuss how we could best support the families and other tutors we work with. Quite a lot of our team are final year Psychology students or recent graduates with an interest in working with children or people with autism. I did not want them, or our students and families, to be put in an even more difficult situation. We contacted all families and tutors and looked at alternatives to visits, opening a dialogue with families to be flexible and safe, whilst still providing the support they needed. We were due to start a six-week-long 'Cadets' course (our social skills Saturday group) the day after the Friday of school closures, but we decided it could not go ahead.

My colleagues and I do not normally work face to face every day. We give feedback to one another in weekly and monthly meetings. We are used to keeping in daily contact through email, phone calls and so on, so in the first week of lockdown we had remote meetings and check-ins, making sure we had been in contact with all our families. We discussed what they thought they needed and what we could offer.

Seb Jefferies

Relationships with colleagues have not really changed. Maybe we have grown closer because we are trying to solve the problem of how to teach in this new way. We were always trying to make the next video or the next quiz. I did not feel I had much time to feel sorry for myself. It is a creative and collaborative school anyway, so people would not get away with just uploading a worksheet for students to work on.

Michael Minas

I think it has been interesting getting to know schools that I had not worked with previously. As a consultant, the relationships with teachers can be transient, and it has been even more challenging to develop relationships remotely. I find it more draining working remotely, to be honest, as the interpersonal side of working with educators is harder to maintain over a screen than face to face. I often feel very drained by the end of a day when I have spent it online presenting or planning with teachers.

Amanda Queiroz Moura

My PhD was about communication, so I am passionate about dialogue and I defended the right to this throughout. I am careful when I ask questions and ensure that students have the opportunity to talk with each other as I believe we learn in the interaction with others. So, it is especially hard for me to not have that interaction. These are things that I believe, so I have to think, 'it's a moment, an experience and I should fit with the situation'. At first, I tried to teach like I do in the classroom, but the students were lost with my methodology, so I talked with my coordinator at school, who said we do not have control over what students are learning, but we need to offer exercises and corrections. Maybe they will want to discuss with you, but if not, we offer the opportunity for learning anyway.

I reflected on this with friends and a therapist which helped and was a different form of relationship with them for me. It made me realise that I understand I need to change. I usually teach face to face, and it works for me; the students feel comfortable with my approach. The current long periods of time of online mathematics is challenging for me, but I am trying to resolve all the problems I am facing. I reassure the students that there is no problem. I am trying to have this kind of dialogue and give emotional support to my students and to find ways of having a dialogue with colleagues that will support me.

Nicodemus Amboko Muhati

The pandemic has had a lot of social effects. People have been affected in one way or the other socially, economically mostly and culturally. A lot of things have changed, and all the social distancing protocols given by the Minister of Health in Kenya have to be followed. When it comes to relationships with colleagues, most of the time these have been very professional. But we also have a life outside the professional world. We have a life outside school because we make friends with people in our work environment. During the weekend we used to go out hiking, having fun, but then you can no longer do that. No-one is still interested in that. Unfortunately, we cannot bond outside because of Covid-19. Life is strange. Life has changed. Life has really changed. Some people are finding they have difficulties with mental health. I have always been someone who enjoys having my kids in class and so I am one of the people who have been affected mental health wise because I find myself glued to the screen from morning to night from Monday to Friday. Sometimes at the end of the day I am completely drained, and I do not want to talk to anybody. Someone can call you and you miss that call, not because you do not want to pick up that call, but because of the situation you are in at the moment.

Betty Sheila Mumbi

I think working from home means you do not get to interact with a lot of people. So, what would have been me just going into a colleague's classroom to ask for help or meeting them on the corridors to ask for help is quite difficult. When I need particular help, I call or send emails, so that is a bit difficult, as opposed to when you could just meet people in the corridor and have a quick chat. And now everyone else is teaching all the time, so we meet either when we are both free or over the weekends, and you can make calls and just chat with each other. There is a colleague in my house (as my school is a boarding school I live here) and normally during working days we would not be spending as much time here because everyone is busy with their life. But now, because of the regulations set out by the government, movement is quite restricted, so you cannot just pop into other peoples' houses and we are spending all the time in our own house.

Hubert Mathanzima Mweli

During this time, the relationships between the Department and education stakeholders have strengthened significantly. We have had countless meetings to plan how we would re-open schools safely for everyone: teachers, learners and support staff alike. Teacher Unions, School Governing Body Associations, Learner formations, the Principals Association, as well as the National Alliance of Independent School Associations (NAISA), have all participated in processes to seek solutions and consensus on the priorities. This experience has demonstrated how every stakeholder is important and plays a critical role in education.

As is the case the world over, there was much concern in South Africa that the re-opening of schools will lead to an increase in new infections. Parents and caregivers rightfully feared for the health of their children, while the staff were concerned of the risk of infection from learners. There were also many opportunistic groupings that took the Department to court or sought to close schools with force. The use of available evidence from renowned public health experts, epidemiologists and paediatrics, coupled with the advice from the Department of Health, assisted the sector to explain its approach and demonstrate its scientifically sound approach.

Helen Toft

It felt very dramatic at first. It felt as though all our jobs in the PGCEi team were under threat because of the impact of the virus on the university's finances. This led to me being uncertain about my future at the institution. It did not feel like the right time to be the end of my career and was very, very, challenging. It felt hard to communicate with anyone about how I was really feeling. It felt very isolating.

At the same time the huge Black Lives Matter (BLM) movement was happening, and colleagues and friends of diverse backgrounds were having even worse experiences in the pandemic because of the terrible political and social traumas that had led to BLM. I wanted to try and support these colleagues and friends and it felt hard to do this when we could not meet up.

Some colleagues' experiences were traumatic. I became very angry about racism and social injustice, as well as the way our country handled the control of the pandemic. It felt like we should not have got to a stage where the impact was so much worse for these colleagues and in minority ethnic people across the UK. I got very involved with trying to support them, became an even more overt ally at work and home. It felt, to me, like it was vital that allies were vocally supporting people who were crushed.

Outside of work, there was one choir session I will never forget when Thanda (the community choir leader in the town) talked so movingly to us about how the BLM movement had impacted him. It was both humbling and empowering. In terms of that choir, I think Thanda and I have become even closer as colleagues and friends because we really were not sure how online singing would work with elderly people, or even if it was possible. There was a massive and quick learning curve about using *Zoom* with the choir and an anxiety about using technology when several members had none. Thanda and I had always planned together, but now we had to plan much more carefully before the sessions. Eventually, some of us took responsibility for 'admin' in the session so that Thanda could focus on the singing, but it took a while to realise how we could do this. I had attended good models of this shared approach to moderating online meetings work, where one person leads the meeting, and another watches the chat so that they can ensure everyone who wants to speak can do; waiting to speak seems to make contributions short and focused.

Back at work, panel meetings about issues to address inequalities for black and Asian colleagues in our institution have been particularly powerful because the whole meeting can see all the panel and how they are interacting as they speak. It seems to make us listen harder. This intense approach has certainly been motivating for me. The online platform allowed black and Asian colleagues from around the country to form the panel without having to travel to the same place. This immediately made access to a diverse panel more practical. It made me realise that using online platforms we can put together an expert panel of people from all around the world relatively easily.

Delmer Tzib

We worked as a department to create the CAP (continuative academic plan), but our usual way of working is to plan and teach our own courses, so this continued. Clearly, the day-to-day direct interaction in our shared office went down. But, we keep in touch through a *WhatsApp* group. We tried to have regular meetings, just to share how it was going in general, and how we were feeling. But this all takes place through *WhatsApp* now rather than through less formal conversations in the office.

The pandemic, or rather our response to the pandemic, has changed the nature of our relationships because we were no longer interacting daily, but we knew we had the support of each other through the *WhatsApp* group. This feeling of a shared responsibility was important. If I had something I wanted to ask a colleague or something I wanted to share I would just post to the group and someone would respond. It was good to sense that we were all looking out for each other.

Another aspect that was important is that our department maintained heavy debate on social issues through the *WhatsApp* group. We all have strong views and the *WhatsApp* group was an avenue to share them and debate. This process enabled us to develop an even stronger bond which helped us to cope with the stresses of all the changes occurring.

Louise Whyte

Within my department, things have not changed too much. Our timetables are a lot busier, but we still manage to see each other quite a lot, and we try to have a weekly meeting or catch up.

I rarely see colleagues from other departments on a regular basis this year due to restrictions and social distancing. When I speak to colleagues from other schools, they say a similar thing, that everybody is with children so much more this year you just do not see many colleagues. Sometimes this is because classes have been split to make them smaller, so timetables have got longer and busier, or because we have many more duties because breaks and lunch times are staggered. If you are not timetabled free with the colleague, you just do not see them.

Some of those corridor conversations that used to solve so many issues instantly have stopped, and everything has moved online. This is often positive as you feel more informed, but it also means you get a constant stream of messages to sift through when you get a chance. I do not really see management as much; meetings are video calls. Almost everything is through electronic communication.

Vicky Van Wyk

As the situation escalated quite quickly, most of my colleagues had left the country. I had to adapt to the notion that coffee mornings and reflections were not applicable at that moment in time. Unfortunately, many people can relate to this. Even though the face-to-face value of conversing was lacking, as teachers we had to come up with lessons that would be exciting and enticing for the little ones, so there was a lot of remote collaboration happening, which I thought was great. Many of my older colleagues had to find a part-time replacement for online teaching as they had a very hard time learning how to conduct lessons through *Zoom* at this stage in their careers, which was unfortunate. The adaption of working from home definitely had its own side effects. I was lucky enough to have a balcony that I could make use of instead of just staying inside all day, but it was quite hard for me to separate work from home, as my apartment had now become my classroom.

Reflections

Perhaps the pandemic magnified the situations that existed for us in our pre-pandemic ways of working with colleagues. When we are busy one of the first things we lose are those day-to-day interactions with colleagues that are so important in making us feel as though we are engaged in a collegial effort of education. Those teams, like Jasmine's, Helen's and Tony's, which already relied on effort being made to support each other as working remotely from each other seemed to be impacted less than the teaching teams which had come to take for granted the informal interactions in offices or on corridors which helped build that feeling of common cause.

And, perhaps, we are still working through how we can resolve issues when we feel in conflict with colleagues that would be much easier to sort out in a face-to-face meeting. There is some suggestion in the stories above that the feeling of a shared responsibility to get this right for our learners meant that we grew closer together. Shared stress and shared problem solving can quickly create a strong group identity. Shared planning means we take responsibility for our colleagues and try to make sure the experience is as positive as possible. This does rely on trust, and Hubert Mweli describes how the South African government prioritised safety for teachers and learners. Learning cannot take place if we do not feel safe in the place in which we are supposed to be learning.

There has been much use of apps like *WhatsApp* as a tool to replace the more informal interactions. Delmer explores the importance of using apps such as this to ensure the team stays close.

What we have all lost, and it does not feel like we have solved this problem yet, is the social element to our relationships with colleagues. Mr Muhati describes all the activities he misses that he would normally be enjoying with his colleagues. Several of the stories reflect on how, after a day working online, we are too tired to go back online to socialise with our colleagues. Perhaps this is something we need to prioritise once we are able to return to schools.

How have your relationships with your colleagues changed? Which of the issues identified above are important for you? Which have not impacted on your relationships?

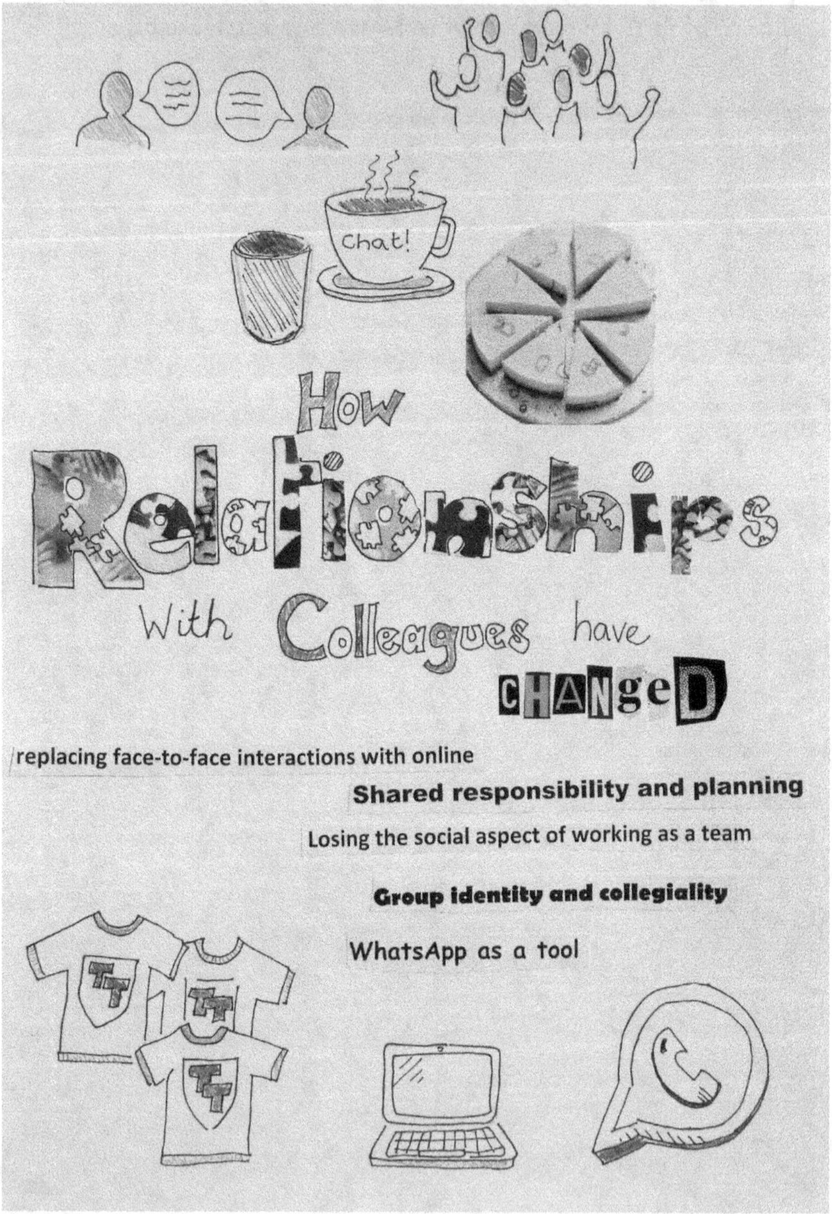
Chat!
How
Relationships
with Colleagues have
CHANGED
replacing face-to-face interactions with online
Shared responsibility and planning
Losing the social aspect of working as a team
Group identity and collegiality
WhatsApp as a tool
TT
TT
TT

Chapter 6

How relationships with learners changed

Introduction

Another thing that change, enforced or otherwise, can do is make us notice things that have otherwise gone unremarked. And, one of the things that we might notice is the ways that people learn. When our everyday practice is suddenly transformed, we begin to notice learning, not just our teaching. It is often useful to step back, during a lesson, and just watch the learners for a few moments. Taking a break from teaching to notice what is happening as a result is beneficial whatever the situation. So, this enforced break, this schism in the everyday relationship between teacher and learners, between teaching and learning put us in a place where we could reassess our relationships with those who see us as teachers.

Lucy Cooker

My relationships with students have almost always been positive and that is not just from me but reported back to me from other members of the wider teaching team. I think now the PGCEi programme is totally online, whereas before the course was blended with an initial face-to-face induction programme followed by online learning, there are many advantages for inclusivity, as many students are joining now who could not join the course before because of childcare or because they could not afford to have travelled and had accommodation to attend the training.

Sometimes after face to face we would get the feedback about 'Too much working in groups' or 'I feel uncomfortable working in groups'. Working using the online platforms means the groups are still working together, but I wonder if some people's interpersonal needs are met better. In previous courses, participants have been running from a

DOI: 10.4324/9781003150596-6

break-out space to grab a cup of coffee before a whole cohort plenary in the main teaching room. Teaching online means that individual participants can grab breaks and refreshments whenever they need them.

When working online, there have been students who have asked to keep their cameras off even in small group work. I do not know why because I did not ask them to put their cameras on, but what it does is give individuals the choice to do this in an online medium. I have checked in with some group work sessions and some groups have gone straight into a meeting and run for half an hour, but others have had a really short meeting moving to 'chat' and covered the main points and then choose to work individually on the ideas in more detail. The participants are choosing a particular approach to engagement or dealing effectively with connection issues. At the face-to-face induction, which can run to over 50 participants, the groups are big enough for some people to get lost in. In the online sessions, they might slip away and perhaps they need to, but it is not a problem as there are recordings for them to catch up with. This gives the students much more flexibility to take control over their learning.

Another benefit of moving online is that we have had a lot more students joining sessions from their school, or even in the car on their commute. It is a real advantage that our students can meet their other commitments in school, not taking four to six days out to travel so they can study somewhere distant from where they live and work. They can carry on with all their family roles as well, caring for elderly relatives or their own children. There is a downside for those who do not feel comfortable if they do not want to share their surroundings, or if it is really busy or noisy in the background.

Tony Cotton

I work with teachers around the world, my students in Bangkok, for example, or participants in professional development workshops in countries such as Belize and Mexico. It is different not having direct contact in those situations. I am trying to understand what teaching and learning looks like when you do not get that sort of direct relationship immediately from the face-to-face teaching, and how that is quite interesting.

When we teach the PGCEi online induction, we give participants the option of having their cameras off, which means I do not even really know if they were in the room, or, if they were, they might have been busy doing something else even if they might have every so often typed a message in the chat. It is hard to know until the end of the year how these changes will have an impact. It may be that we get to know our students better over time, as we meet them online through the year, rather than having an intense four-day session at the start of the course.

One thing that I have noticed is that if I open up the chat before the session starts, I can have that informal conversation that I would have prior to a face-to-face session. In fact, this is more effective using the 'chat' function as I am always a bit reluctant to start up conversations with students I have never met but for some reason found it easier using a chat bar. Particularly for the big international webinars I am able to connect to people from countries I have visited or would like to visit.

I also want to reflect on what I have learned from 'teaching' my grandsons, Felix and Tate, online. They both very quickly learned how to use *Zoom* as a communication tool, and we were able to be playful before and after sessions. They quickly realised that they could go off camera to find something or to get something to show me and that this would be a benefit to the session. I have taught Felix how to use the 'chat' bar and the annotation tool in *Zoom*. In this way we can annotate each other's documents, in a way we probably would not do in the flesh. I think I am finding new ways of working all the time and thinking about how I can use these tools when we are through this period.

Edward Emmet

I think the relationships with children and their parents mostly became a lot better, with a few of them much worse, which I will talk about later. A few parents did refuse to pay to attend online lessons, so we lost four students, but colleagues told me that their classes actually gained some children, which was great for the finances of the school, but teachers and kids did not know one another which was quite stressful for both.

For the younger children, I would say online teaching was better for children who were socially advanced. They really enjoyed seeing all their friends, learning how to 'mute' and 'unmute' to join in the lesson. The shy ones struggled, so I asked them to say what they thought about the lesson. The children were easy to control online, just as easy as in the classroom; in some ways they had more confidence. We changed a lot of learning activities around, used a lot more media and we asked questions, but everything a lot slower. I usually had 20 students in my class and every one of them wanted to be involved.

My children are five years old, but they really enjoyed learning about Queen Elizabeth I. I would choose to ask a question of a shyer child, but all hands went up (using the online tool). Parents were watching this and would ask that I include everyone all the time, so lessons were dragged out. I came up with a strategy to use a wheel spin to ask a person, but it kept 'freezing', so then I chose children at random, a good example of technology making me adapt and think on my feet.

One example of how challenging it was is that some children forgot to mute, but the worst case was a Chinese child who knew very little English and kept taking over as 'presenter' and then the lesson would become that family chattering. I asked the assistant to write in Chinese across the screen to stop taking control, but for the whole lesson the children would come on to say there was Chinese all over their screen; what a distraction!

Jessica Greenbaum

It has been interesting that some students I work with who are on the autistic spectrum are happier in remote learning. They do not have to work out all the social cues or get stressed by the social situations they have to deal with in the classroom. For some parents it has been a real tug of war to get them back to school and then, of course, schools shut again.

As teachers we were aware that for students with Autism Spectrum Condition (ASC), the massive amount of change and uncertainty had the potential to have a more severe impact. As a result, we made our online programme very routine and predictable. For example, in mathematics, each Monday we introduced a new game, Tuesday was a flipped classroom style lesson, Wednesday was a number talk and problem-based learning, Thursday was 'Mathletics' and Friday was 'Maths in the Home'. It was very predictable, and this was intentional, particularly for those students with additional needs.

When we finally returned to onsite learning in Term 4 (October 2020), I anticipated that those students would struggle with the transition back into the classroom. Interestingly, the majority of students with ASC coped really well. I believe this was in part due to our whole-school approach, which was a primary focus on well-being (directed by the Department of Education). We treated the time very much like it was the beginning of a new school year. It was in fact those students with mild anxiety pre-Covid-19 (not necessarily those with ASC) who struggled most. Their anxiety became emphasised, and they were the ones who struggled more so with the transition to and from remote learning.

Jasmine Irani

One child got bored of *Zoom* and walked off and then closed the iPad. I was using all of the strategies of a face-to-face session to motivate them, such as helping them to recognise their feelings and prompting them to take a break if they were feeling frustrated. Now I am seeing how there are options for these strategies even over *Zoom*, reflectivity can be built in, we can still play and take breaks within the *Zoom session*. I think I was too anxious at first that the children still had to 'get through' lots of learning activities, but quickly recognised, that like in face-to-face sessions, if you have not spent time building good relationships and trust, then it is very difficult to get any 'work' done!

Seb Jefferies

The kids love to speak English to me; that is what they want to do, so they will phone me on *google hangouts* just to speak English. I also think that our relationships have grown closer. Although, to be honest, relationships have always been close between students and teachers. It seems to be a Mongolian thing, a really strong bond between students and teachers.

The kids have been incredibly resilient. I was really impressed with how quickly they adjusted to the new situation. They just seemed to get on with it. It was the same with the parents as well. There has always been a very close parent community with the school. Parents would help out with plays and performances, with sports days and things like that.

Several parents have become the film crew for their children. They have produced very nicely edited and really well put together videos to upload, showing their children's responses to the activities. These videos just come to me for privacy issues. We needed to keep the videos private. The Mongolian law on children's rights is really strict. For photographs or videos, the child has to give permission as well as both parents. It is interesting to me that children's rights are enshrined in Mongolian law.

Children and learning are very important here. There are children's palaces – a centre where children can go for extra-curricular activities. I wonder if this comes from the Russian tradition. They go to these palaces to learn traditional instruments or the traditional script. There are two traditional scripts, Cyrillic and the Mongolian script, which is very different. There is a big push in the country at the moment for children to learn the traditional script.

I am interested that in some ways people in the territories that were invaded by Genghis Khan had more freedom, women had rights and children had rights. The societies he created were more egalitarian in some ways. This is not the story that we hear about or read about in history books.

Michael Minas

Some of the schools that I worked with started off in our first lockdown with teachers trying to teach the whole day, live online. Some other schools had no live contact between students and teachers at all.

We are now in our second lockdown and the second time around it feels like schools now have a more consistent approach, which is probably the result of getting more direction, in terms of what works. The first time around, schools were left to figure it out for themselves. This time round schools have had more guidance. For example, most schools across our state have introduced an initial morning meeting, at around 9 am each day.

I think for students these morning meetings are more about seeing their peer's faces, making informal contact and thus maintaining social connections. Nash, my six-year-old son, is collecting books as part of a supermarket promotion and via his morning meetings he discovered that so are many of his friends. They find time in the morning meeting to let each other know which books they are missing. The other day I heard a knock on the door and the dad of one of Nash's friends had brought round some of the books that we were missing. Little things like this have helped to make students feel like they are still part of a community.

Amanda Queiroz Moura

As I said before, one of my jobs is teaching mathematics to students of Catholic traditional middle class who live in my region. I started teaching online without having met the students face to face. In this school the families do not have social or economic problems. Most families have computers and a camera and microphone, but the students do sometimes choose not to open the camera. It was especially difficult for me not to have live interactions with the students as I value dialogue and discussion in the classroom. These are things that I believe, so I have to think 'this period is just a moment, a new and different experience and I should fit in with the situation'. At first, I tried to teach like I do in the classroom, but the students did not understand my methodology, so I talked with my coordinator at school who said we do not have control over what students are learning, but we do need to offer exercises and corrections. Maybe they will want to discuss with you, but if not we offer the opportunity for learning anyway.

My first day as a teacher in the high school was the first day of lockdown in São Paulo city. For these reasons, I did not meet my students face to face, which resulted in some problems of communication and adaptation with methods of teaching. My relationships with the students did not go beyond introducing activities and making corrections to their work. Throughout the year they did not open the camera or use a microphone to say something; almost all of the questions were by chat. I tried to maintain the same style of class and the same routine weekly, which helped the students to understand more of the content, however without dialogue or in-depth interactions. Not having the usual interaction with the students was a very weird experience and certainly influenced our relationship.

Nicodemus Amboko Muhati

Ordinarily, you find a teacher who is seen as a 'surrogate parent'. I always believe being a teacher is a calling. There is a gap that you fill, something that you do, which not even a parent can do. And these children always find a lot of comfort and a lot of warmth under the wings of a teacher.

Now many of our students have suffered when it comes to mental health issues. As a member of the Committee on Guiding and Counselling, I find that there are a lot of issues coming up. Mostly, I will find a child will come and complain and say these days I don't even feel like coming to school online because I always want to meet in person. And, I want to meet the child in person because that makes me feel so happy. So, things have changed now in the way you used to know this child. Things have changed in the participation in learning. It may be that things appear fine on Monday, and then something changes on Wednesday, so that by Thursday and Friday they will be a totally different child. It is not because the child does not want to learn but because this child is hitting a low. It is because there is something that the child is missing. When you engage with somebody one on one, in person, there is a way you feel happy. There is a way you feel satisfied, that you know you really have taught them something by the end of the day. The child goes home remembering that Mr Hottie has really made a great impact in my life.

I use play-based learning and a range of teaching methods for each of my children. I am delivering the same content, but they are learning in different ways. If I need them to explain a concept, it might be that one child wants to draw cartoons and annotate them with comment bubbles explaining the concepts. This approach still gives answers to the same question. Then there will be the child who is good at writing poems or singing and rapping in class. So, they can take this approach. The content is still the same.

I remember discussing visual, auditory and kinaesthetic learning styles. I was trying to introduce this idea but, at times, I do not have the opportunity to do this because online time means I have very little time with these children. Normally after school the children can access my office. They can chat, chat with you, chat about things that are not even necessarily within the curriculum, but they have something that they said they want to chat with you at the end of the day. This can also make a difference in the life of a child. So, you see relationships between teachers and students have also changed a lot, yeah? It is such an important part of any interaction between students and teachers, where you know they come and see you after class just to check their understanding. Unfortunately, right now this cannot happen.

One of the issues that have arisen is that the amount of time that a child spends onscreen has to be limited. Normally school starts at 7:45 and ends at 3:30 and all through this time the children have been on the screen. It is not fair, so parents requested, and the school agreed, that children need to have a break from the screen. So ordinarily, I might extend a lesson for 10 minutes because they are enjoying an activity, but I can no longer do that.

Betty Sheila Mumbi

Normally when students are in school, you get to meet pretty much all the students in the prep school at one point or another. Now if they are not in your teaching group, you probably do not get to interact with them at all. You are limited to students who are in your teaching groups and not the entire school, as would normally be the case. Assemblies are still done in *Teams*, live assemblies and we have what we call live masterclasses. They are cross-curricular, so all kids get to be part of it. They participate in whatever activities are being done, so the kids still get to interact with each other.

Hubert Mathanzima Mweli

The South African Government declared hard lockdown between March and April 2020, literally taking learners and teachers out of the classroom/onsite learning. In our education system, the comfort of teaching and learning is entrenched in the classroom and the lockdown disrupted that routine, spinning the education sector into new ways of learning. The new ways of learning included radio broadcast of lessons, streamed lessons through Television and Telematic platforms, Dial-a-Tutor and Web-based applications that provided resources to learners while at home. Schools with resources were able to resort to full-scale e-learning. In most public schools communication between the teachers and the learners was reduced and that reduced effective learning.

Helen Toft

I think one of my strengths is the way I can make connections with all my learners in a deep way. It feels like the pandemic has made the connections even closer because when you now ask, 'How are you?' it carries a different weight. It is a much more powerful and meaningful question, and the answer is more important. Many of my students have got family that they have created in SE Asia, but also have family in the UK or the US and many other countries, which have been hard hit by the virus. They are very concerned about what the virus is doing in these countries. I think several of my students saw me as a link to that concern and so I became important to them in that way.

I think they found it reassuring to talk to me and I felt reassured by the conversations too. This was probably helped by the fact that quite a lot of my students are a bit older than traditional university students.

I also had some experience of working with my then seven-year-old grandson in his music performance workshops with Thanda, my South African locally based choir leader, using *Zoom*. That was joyous, fairly chaotic, but a lot of fun. This was a different form of my relationship with Felix because I think he rarely thinks of me as a teacher. And this was an opportunity for Felix to be taught one to one by Thanda from a totally different town, that would not have happened if not for lockdown.

I also made sure that those members of the choir who cannot access *Zoom* were okay, by visiting them, passing on what we have been doing and handing out packs Thanda produced about his background and song writing inspired by migration. One member of the choir died unexpectedly (not of Covid-19) and many members attended her funeral by lining the street for her passing. Previously one or two representatives would have gone to a funeral, but this felt like many more of us actually physically attended the drive by. It was a shocking and somehow more communally shared event in a situation which made 'community' hard to participate in.

Delmer Tzib

I think that our immediate reaction to the school shutdown, which entailed having students work online (without cameras or voice interaction) was not fruitful. We were learning and as such we managed to change the plan as we went along. I wanted the students to know that I was there for them; I wanted the students to see me as supportive, rather than someone who was trying to police their online presence. The Ministry of Education told us that none of the online work should be graded; anything that the students submitted could only be used as evidence to increase their grade level. No student's grade level could go down as a result of their participation in online learning. If a student does not engage at all, does not submit anything, their grade will stay the same as it was when schools were closed. I think this is hard for my 'A' grade students, because they cannot get a higher grade. They are submitting more and more for their grade to stay the same. It seems to be the students who really need to increase their grades who do not always submit and work or engage in online learning.

I am not sure my relationship with my students has changed very much as the relationships had already been built in school. I have the same relationship with my students as I had before. I have had tons of emails from the students just asking about the situation, asking questions about the situation in general. This has given me a sense of importance and a sense of responsibility to support them.

When the academic year 2020–2021 started the dynamics were different. We had a clearer vision and had a more structured way of interacting. The live sessions certainly brought the 'in class' feeling alive. The students concentrated more and performed better in their classes.

Louise Whyte

The first couple of weeks back in school after lockdown were really nice. The kids had clearly missed being away a lot more than they said they had and so everyone was glad to be back and there was a really jovial atmosphere. And then we had to start getting through the curriculum again!

I would not say relationships between teachers and students have changed too much. I think they feel like we care a lot more than before, although of course we have always cared! We check in with them a lot, but I do not know if we should keep asking them if they are okay. They have demonstrated that they are adaptable and have adjusted to the new school situation remarkably well. For many of us, we are facing quite a tough decision. I think if I went to work and every day my manager asked, 'How are you doing today? Are you OK? Are you feeling stressed?', I would start panicking a bit.

We have all been through something quite tough and we are all just trying our best, so I think there is a bit of a closer relationship. We learn and make mistakes in a way which is more understanding; there is a little bit more trust. It is quite a comfortable relationship.

However, we do have to keep reminding students of the rules and that is getting a bit tricky; there is some resistance. In the morning they are okay, but by the afternoon they become a bit restless about the restrictions.

When we were teaching online, it was quite common for children to refuse to show their faces on camera, and as a school we decided not to enforce that, because to be honest, we did not truly know what the personal situation was like for a lot of them. We knew that some students were using inadequate devices or had no camera and might have been in a room with three siblings that were also doing online lessons, but unfortunately, some had difficult family situations and faced very challenging circumstances. We knew that some of them had a more valid reason for not having the camera on. Consequently, we did not treat cameras off as a disciplinary matter; we just had to get on with it. On Monday mornings I had Year 10 for an hour online and only one or two cameras would be turned on and it was really difficult. You did not know how fast they were working through an activity or if they were struggling or getting bored. It was a pretty weird experience. Normally, as teachers, we work with constant feedback, so having that taken away was really difficult.

Vicky Van Wyk

I tried my best to maintain the relationship I had with the students, prior to the lockdown, trying to check in and see how they are doing. However, parents made this quite hard as there was a continuous presence in the classroom; thus children were more reluctant to speak up. I tried to create a fun, interactive way to check in, based on the answers of the students. My face-to-face check-in would be focused on their mental health, home life and if they were alright at home. Doing this online was a bit trickier, so I had to adapt to the way I was interacting with them, asking different questions based on if they have read their favourite book or have done their favourite activity, or what they ate for lunch. It was apparent if this was lacking, it may have been a form of punishment. Sadly, I am unsure how much they comprehended as there was a language barrier and were quite young as well.

Reflections

It appears as though working online using any of the many online platforms that have flourished during lockdown has offered a flexibility that we were not expecting. Particularly for older learners it allows them to be flexible in where they learn; they can choose a space that they find suitable and when they learn. They can stop online presentations and return to them when they need to or repeat sections that they want to revisit. The chat function also allows learners to decide whether they want to ask everyone a question or just ask the teacher. This can be less exposing for a learner. The break-out groups' functions also hand over some control to groups as to how they might work. Are we beginning to see a slight shift in the power dynamic between the teacher and the learner through the use of online platforms?

A flip side to this is that it seems to be harder to make direct contact with individuals in the way that we do in face-to-face sessions. We cannot have a private chat before or after sessions if we pick up the signs of something being wrong. Although we were able to maintain social connections in other ways, Helen introducing teachers who would not have been available for face-to-face teaching; Nash's friends popping round to swap books they were collecting and the insights into each other's spaces we have all experienced. In some sense we have all been invited into each other's homes over the last year or so and have shared our learning spaces. Again, this seems like a subtle shift in the power dynamic. The teacher no longer controls the learning space. Perhaps the clearest evidence of this is Jasmine's learner literally closing the screen down.

There are a few frustrations, and it is clear that all learners need support, need teaching how to use the platforms. Some of the stories wonder if it is easier for older children to use these platforms. Maybe, or perhaps they just use them in different ways to younger learners. As with lots of things we can probably learn from watching how our youngest learners use the platforms. There is lots of advice on using tools such as 'hands-up', allowing individuals to ask questions using the chat function and advice on muting and not muting. A friend who lectures at a university insists that he is going to tell his students in his face-to-face lectures that he is 'putting you all on mute'.

An important issue that these stories raise is that of inclusion. Could it be that online learning is more inclusive? Some of these sessions were certainly easier to access for teachers and students all around the world. So, having the money for travel was not a requirement for access to online learning. Similarly, learners could fit sessions around other caring or work responsibilities. Jess noticed that some of her students with an assessment of ASC were happier in remote learning. Although Jasmine, a specialist in this area, reminds us that relationships are paramount when working with any learner. Mr Muhati also makes sure we do not forget the importance of well-being and of looking after the mental health of our learners. A part of this is finding ways to limit screen time; we cannot just expect our learners to look at a screen for the same amount of time as they would have been in a classroom. Similarly, our practice will not be more inclusive if we do not find ways to use a wide range of learning and teaching strategies. We need to remember that our learners are all individuals and need to learn and respond in many different ways to our teaching.

Finally, what shines through is the resilience of our learners. In many ways it is this that has kept us going. We must not take this for granted, however, or use it as an excuse for our own shortcomings. We always need to remember to find ways to check in with our learners to make sure they are okay, and to check in with ourselves to ensure we are looking after our own well-being.

Personal reflection on 'how relationships with learners changed'.

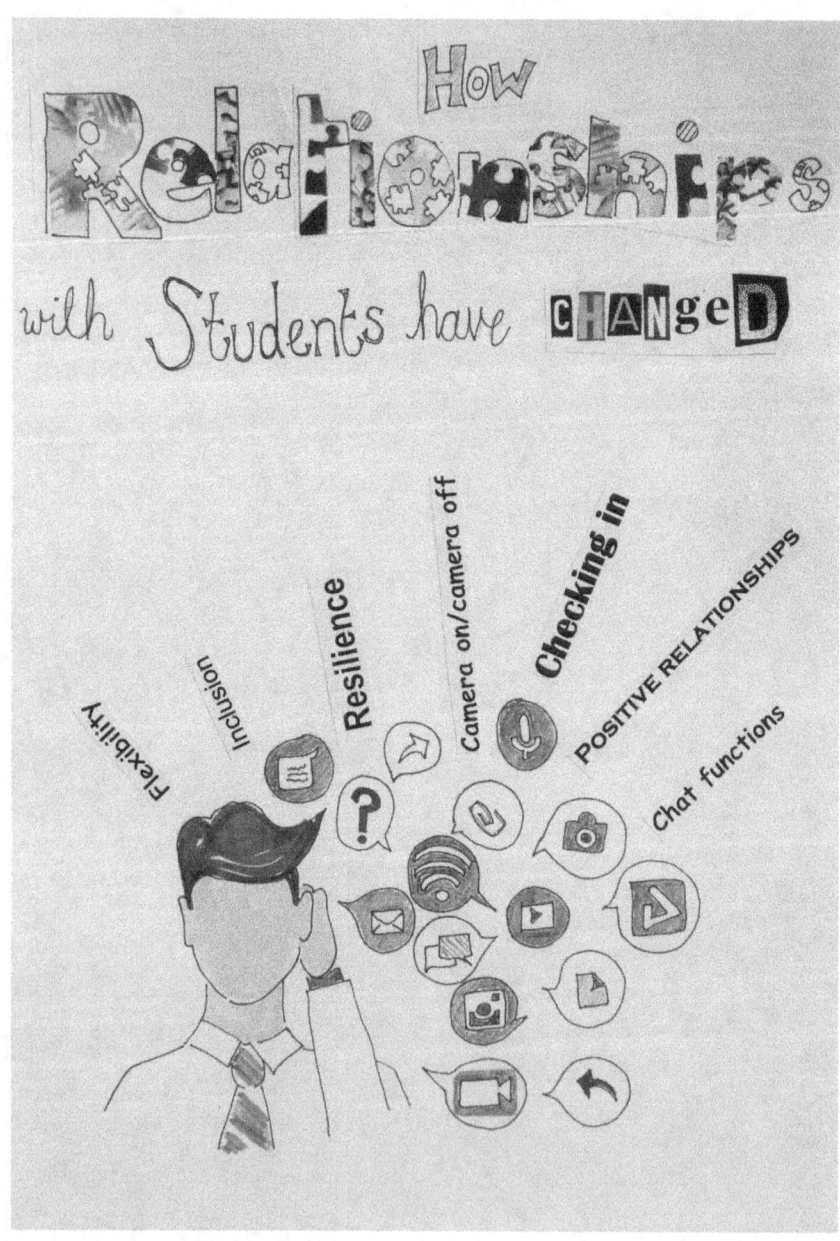

Chapter 7

How relationships with parents and the wider community changed

Introduction

It was interesting that the first response for many of us as we started to put this together was to suggest that there was no relationship with parents or community to build on or to develop. This was a little surprising as several of the teacher colleagues who are contributing had commented on the constant presence of parents whilst online learning was taking place, or of the expectations that parents had placed on the schools in terms of the content of the online learning sessions. In fact, Lucy, Helen and Tony revisited this chapter both for themselves and with their co-authors. Clearly, and uncontroversially, education should involve parents and the community, but how can this be done when schools are closed.

Lucy Cooker

In my new role I do not have contact with parents or the wider community, particularly in Nottingham. I used to interact with the wider community globally on behalf of the PGCEi setting up new cohorts in cities or schools around the world, but that is not my role anymore.

Tony Cotton

When I started teaching Felix, my grandson, and his friends, some of the mums (they were all mums) wanted a *WhatsApp* group and I was sharing activities for them to do. Most of these activities required parental involvement, and I explained that these were not just activities to

DOI: 10.4324/9781003150596-7

keep children busy and quiet, but I needed them to become involved with their children. Predominantly, people really enjoyed what we were doing, and the ones that did get involved really enjoyed it. There were probably one or two who said, 'Thanks very much, but I'm going to download Purple Maths (a commercially available mathematics education programme) because my child can just get on with that'. These parents saw the purpose of home schooling as being something to keep the kids quiet. In particular, I think quite often people have a view of mathematics as something that keeps you busy. Whereas had it been a craft activity, I can imagine they might be happier to get involved. I would argue that even if you have several children being home schooled you can involve everybody in the same activities even, and perhaps especially, if it is mathematics. It was great when parents sent round images of the responses to the activity that their child had been involved with. One parent posting a photo on the *WhatsApp* group would encourage other parents to do the same.

I think that because I was drawing on more open-ended activities, which allowed the children to respond at different levels, the parents began to see mathematics slightly differently. Previously the only model of mathematics that they could draw on was their own experience at school; now they were seeing different possibilities. Disappointingly, during the second period of lockdown the school has sent home a workbook for Felix to work through with the requirement that he complete three pages a day. Mathematics has turned from something he used to explore with his friends and used to involve parents to a task to be completed as quickly as possible. This shows how much impact the selection of activities can have on the home-schooling experience.

Edward Emmet

I would like to expand on what I wrote earlier about the relationship with parents starting off really badly. Many of the parents were annoyed about teaching online because they had to do such a lot with their children at home. My class was the youngest age group being taught online and so perhaps the parents of this age group found supporting them at home the most difficult. As I mentioned earlier, some families left the school, but those who stuck around made an amazing compilation for me in an online 'taskmaster' challenge; they would have won the competition if they had sent them in to Alex Horne's TV programme (a UK-based comedy programme – look up #hometasking on *Twitter* if you are interested).

But absolutely the best thing was that I told the parents to read a lot with their children and sent links for them to buy books online, and by the end of lockdown I had five children go up to level 7, 8 and 9 instead of being on the usual 4, 5 and 6.

Jessica Greenbaum

I have to say that I have had lots of really, really positive experiences with parents. I have a real sense that whatever I put out there should say something about what I value about learning and teaching. Everything we send out, as teachers, sends the message, 'This is what we value'. I think we have taken this opportunity to educate the parents about why we do what we do. I have just had parent interviews back at school and these were really positive. Lots of the parents said, 'Now I finally understand what you are doing at school'.

So, for example, the mathematics in a week might be a game from Michael on Monday for the children to play with their parents and mathematics in the home task the next day. The activities are really open ended and encourage the children (and their parents) to see the mathematics around them every day.

Jasmine Irani

I ran parents' sessions over *Zoom*, to talk them through activities they could do with their child, that was really good. With the particular needs of the children we teach, parental support is really important. In an ideal world parents would always be running activities with their children as we do during sessions, but this does not always happen due to busy parents and conflicting responsibilities. But during lockdown, for some families, it gave them more time to do those things; they had hours to fill. We had the time to talk them through. Now we're going back to face-to-face teaching the parents have a deeper understanding of where their child is and this empowers them to feel confident doing things or adapting things for their child.

I did lose touch with one family, though this was not because of the technology being a problem. Their child was still attending school, because in the UK children with EHCPs (Education, Health and Social

Care Plans) were still entitled to go, and they had access to respite care. They did not want after-school sessions, due to the risk of infection (if they had to self-isolate their child would not be able to attend school or respite care), so this has impacted us being part of their support network.

Parents did not use *Zoom* before and we made the teams they were in smaller. We made sure that the team meetings were not too big. This meant there were a few more meetings to fit in, but on the plus side whilst partners normally met once a month, we were now meeting once a week, so this increased the time we had to talk.

Seb Jefferies

I wrote earlier about how resilient the children were, how well they coped with all the changes taking place. It was the same with the parents. I suppose there has always been a very close parent community with the school. They have always been very keen to help out with plays and performances, with sports days and things like that. I also wrote about how the parents put together the videos for their children to share. But, all of this came through the children.

Amanda Queiroz Moura

I do not have a relationship with parents, but a mother came into a meeting, critiquing my methodology, which was very embarrassing. I just gave her my calm replies, I recorded the meeting and sent it to the head, and they talked with her.

I was teaching in a private school, where education is seen as a product and the parents are our clients, most of them from the middle class. The managers in the school were concerned with providing a good education for the students, but mainly, an education that the parents could agree on. As they are seen as clients, the opinion of the parents about our classes was very important to the school. However, the school did not give the chance for teachers like me to talk with the parents, to explain my goals and methods. The community is very important to me and I imagine that during online classes, it is important to try to construct something together, so the parents understand that they also have a role in the education of the students. Together we can decide what could be better for all. I think, in my school, this connection was lacking.

Michael Minas

I think during the first lockdown there was a fear of expecting too much involvement of parents. The second time around, there was a sense that the parents have to get involved in order to make the learning work. We cannot just chuck the kid a booklet or sit them in front of a tablet and ask them to get on with it. I think there will be some kids who will come out of this stronger. They have learned to manage their time; to be resilient and they have parents who are willing and able to spend the extra time with them. It's a fine line, though, because many parents are also trying to juggle their own responsibilities as well, which has created a lot of stress for families during this time.

Interestingly I have had more requests from schools to run events for the community around mathematics since the pandemic started. I think the schools may have learned that engaging the community in learning mathematics is important. One of the interesting things is that despite having lots of schools interested in hosting this type of event, many have held off on organising one, as they want to wait until restrictions ease in order to allow them to have the largest group of parents/families possible attend.

When planning for these sessions, I ask the staff members I am working with what their number one aim is, and ultimately it comes back that they want to help their families so that they will know how to best support the students in maths. Many schools are already aware of the gap between parent comfort level when it comes to supporting their child's language development as opposed to offering help in maths.

So, guided by this goal, we normally design the sessions to be as hands on as possible. Often this will involve teaching the families a range of maths games that they can play at home, with each game selected on the basis that it is mathematically rich, simple to play, has scope for easy differentiation and requires minimal equipment, thus making it easy to play at home. It is through the act of playing these games that many parents realise just how much learning can take place. The sessions can also include a brief intro on how mathematics is taught at the school, usually by exploring a typical lesson. I also encourage schools to include some time for questions and answer sessions.

One of the schools I work with is planning on holding a regular, fortnightly maths afternoon, where families can come after picking up their child and explore hands-on activities designed to be used at home. Each session will have a theme, for example, place value games, so parents can decide which sessions are most applicable for their child.

Nicodemus Amboko Muhati

In terms of the school community, we used to have what we call family lunch sessions. For example, for Year 9, you will find a teacher has been assigned as a mentor to two or three students. Family lunch was the time when we could all have lunch together. In the dining hall, the mentor and the mentees are seated there, chatting and enjoying lunch, talking about things. It is a time when children can express themselves in a relaxed environment and discuss whatever they like. It doesn't have to be about biology or history. We may decide today we are going to talk about academic issues, and they might say, 'Sir I'm having this challenge, what can I do?'. We would discuss this in the way we would if we were a family, because we are a family of mentor and mentees.

Now, since the pandemic, we can no longer have lunch because the government has ruled that even if the school is open, no meals can be prepared. The children have to come to school with their lunch and you cannot be together with them because there is a separate area which has been set aside for them to have lunch. You cannot really enjoy a conversation as a family because with two metres social distancing you will be shouting. So, those moments have gone.

Thinking about a different aspect of the school community, we have members of staff who are not teachers, who are not classroom specialists. Unfortunately, for example, you look at a school, not necessarily my school, but you look at a school and you see people have lost jobs. A school no longer needs that cook. A school no longer needs that driver. People have been laid off and those relationships that have been built over time have suddenly gone. These people now have nothing to eat. I miss those people. They miss me. We miss each other's company. At school, you may regularly see one of the drivers, for example, and you are always happy talking to this person. You can share anecdotes and stories; then you move away feeling a little bit better inside. Those moments are no longer there.

Now with regard to parents. A parent can come to school and even enter a class for 15–20 minutes just to catch up and follow up on the progress of the child, which is really good practice because parental involvement is very important. Unfortunately, the only opportunity to meet the parents now is online. If the parent has to come to school, you can only meet them outside the gates. There are restrictions, so you have to stay about three metres apart and the maximum amount of time you can engage each other is ten minutes, because you have to go back to school and give attention to the kids. That may not really suffice because, usually, I have a lot of things to report to the parents about the progress their children are making. For that reason, if you have to meet a parent it is only online most of the time. They can book a one-hour consultation slot with you. The parents do not really like these online meetings.

Betty Sheila Mumbi

Relationships between teachers and parents and the community have changed because you are now limited to meeting parents in your particular group. Now I just meet parents to my tutees, whereas before we would meet different parents on sports day or when they are around the school, or when they just come to visit the kids. But now I only meet my six and another tutor meets their parents, and another tutor meets their parents. So, who you meet is very limited.

I do not think the quality of the interaction has changed because we are still discussing the child's progress. I think the only difference is we are now discussing progress from a different perspective. Whereas before we would be discussing the child with them at our side, now we are discussing the child with them at their parent's side. We are still informing the parent about their child's progress because when we are looking at academic progress, it is us, the teachers, who know what the child has been up to. We are the ones reading their notebooks. Most of the parents might be at work or not around the kids, so they do not get to see much of what the child does. So, we are the ones with all that information, and we are feeding it back to them, although they have the child next to them.

Hubert Mathanzima Mweli

Experiences varied amongst parents at times, evoking frustration and duty-care. This ranged from parents who had relied on our National School Nutrition (feeding) Programme (NSNP) and could not feed their children to parents who were just not used to have their children around and had to deal with associated challenges. Parents of learners with special education needs who relied on therapists and specialists were left frustrated as school-based support teams were not available while other community support structures were closed as well. There were, however, some communities that arranged feeding programmes for needy learners and when lockdown eased, the Department had to prioritise psychosocial support to both teachers and learners.

Helen Toft

As a university lecturer I do not usually have a direct relationship with the families of my students, but because I believe in knowing a student well in order to teach them well, they will often mention their family circumstances in conversation about their education history. During what we in the UK refer to as 'the first lockdown' (as I write we are in the third), many students asked for 'extenuating circumstances' to hand their essays in a little later. Sometimes this was because of extra stress at home, for example, many students whose parents and families were being directly impacted by the intense stress of, say, an elderly parent catching Covid-19 early on, when underlying health issues were more likely to cause complications beyond current medical understandings. This occurred with students living and working in China, Nepal and Thailand who had parents respectively in different US states and the UK. The fear caused by long-distance worries suddenly came into sharp focus and studying became just too much pressure. Fortunately, our university had recognised the many complications the pandemic was causing for every student and showed genuine compassion and understanding, which as a personal tutor felt hugely supportive.

As a community volunteer I think I had less impact, even though we tried to help our choir members access the relevant technology in order to take part in weekly sessions. There were many issues involved, especially when those others are even more ill at ease than myself and are at 'arms-length' through a window making it near impossible. Not being able to be in close contact made the whole process feel unwieldy and frustrating for all. Families in what the UK called 'support bubbles' might want to help, but they were adjusting to the demands of the various lockdowns and had many other worries. The local elderly support team were very willing but faced the same issues. By lockdown three, almost one year into the pandemic in the UK, we have three members aged between 80 and 91 trying to access weekly meetings of the choir, with varying degrees of success. In this example the IT has been such a severe issue that the company and joy of participating has been all but lost for some, though we still aim to contact them in some form every now and then.

And finally, as a granny, I was locked in most recently with our daughter's family for three weeks to help when their third baby was born. Witnessing what the demands of home school were like in this situation, even as someone who thinks of herself as an educator through and through, was challenging. Soothing a new baby, playing with a three-year-old having difficulties adapting to that new baby, alongside an eight-year-old with five hours of formal lessons to complete each day with photographic evidence sent to his class teacher at 3.30 pm every day. All this happening in one room with not very up-to-date IT. There was all the noise of each other, with all the adults still responsible for their own businesses and in my case online teaching. The children's school and pre-school were very understanding; all the adults in the family very willing and the children often really enjoyed and engaged with the learning. But as we enter what is now nearly six months of home schooling, I think we should as a country have been more creative with our expectations of untrained parents trying to teach a formal curriculum, and with giving access to easy IT equipment and affordable connectivity to any who need it, no matter what age. One idea might be for local secondary schools to pair up a young person with an older person to act as an IT mentor. This would combat loneliness is many different ways.

Delmer Tzib

Some parents have messaged me. They are showing interest in online learning. But some parents know very little about how the online learning will take place. Many were open to having six sessions per day as the school outlined and the plan that the school proposed was efficient in detailing the structure. Parents supported live sessions; some are event active supervisors for their children. Certainly, this online venture has brought greater parent participation; they are more engaged and involved in their children's development. The email which used to be available but was not used that much, at least in my case, has become a dynamic method of communication. Everything at the fingertips and the parents are more engaged. They seem to think we should try to replicate what we do in school on the internet. For me, this is a different situation, and we need to do things differently.

Louise Whyte

I think parents are able to communicate directly with teachers a lot more as a result of the pandemic. I am not sure if that is always a good thing! The school was already working to improve communication using technology and the plan always was that we would have a new school platform this year, and this just happened to coincide with the return to school. When we were in lockdown, we had quite an archaic way of messaging students and parents. Students did not have *Teams* accounts before we went into lockdown. Parents did not know which platform they should be using as children in secondary had to log into *Teams*, primary used *See Saw* and early years had to access another platform. It was very confusing, and I think many parents had concerns. There is now a very good platform where parents can communicate easily with members of our administrative staff who then deal with these as appropriate. We as teachers can communicate with parents with regards to grades and homework more easily. There is a simple calendar function where we input anything, including grades, attendance and attitude and I think parents really appreciate that level of detail. I think many parents did not know what to do in lockdown. I think they felt like they had a large responsibility to now educate their children. I don't think they understood that actually we had everything planned and all we needed them to do was try and get their child to sign in and then ask them about what they had learnt. During lockdown, parents become more involved in their children's education, so now so many of them are, we cannot lose that involvement.

Vicky Van Wyk

It was clear from the beginning of the lockdown that some parents were not used to being at home with their children. From emails and phone calls I was receiving on either advice on how to help with reading or common parenting activities, it was clear there was a huge gap in parenting skills for some families. In my opinion, I hope this created a realisation for parents on how much love and care their children require, and that there was a dire need for it, now more than ever. Saying this, there was a lot more two-way communication between teachers and parents which had a positive outlook. This interaction made it possible for parents to become more involved with their children, the school and the class teachers, creating a good flow of teamwork amongst the school and families.

Reflection

This chapter has raised the question, 'What role should teachers have with parents and with the wider community, whatever form that community may take?' For this group of educators, the community might be the schools or families of schools for teachers in international schools; community and faith groups for schools that act as community hubs and parents and carers for all teachers in school. The lack of direct contact saw an end to community initiatives such as the family lunch at Mr Muhati's school. How can we replicate this sort of event when schools are closed? Hubert Mweli reminds us that it is the role of education and schools to support families with their most basic of needs, such as making sure that families have sufficient food to eat. There are many stories in England, and I imagine internationally, about the ways in which schools have made sure that the most vulnerable of their learners are cared for.

As we began to write these final reflections a news report came out in the UK suggesting that parents were becoming more aware of the curriculum that their children were following. In England the English curriculum has become quite formal, introducing technical terms for grammar early in a child's education. Some parents were complaining to schools about this and asking about what the point was of knowing such technical terms at the expense of enjoying reading and writing. It seems as though many of the parents of the learners we work with have become more educated about both the curriculum their children follow and the ways of working that are encouraged by the schools. Ed gives the example of parents getting involved with reading which led to improvement in their children's reading skills. Jess reflects on the parents who said to her, 'Now I finally understand what you do at school'. Delmer has seen increased engagement from parents, particularly as the schools in Belize moved into a second lockdown. And Michael gives details of how he showed parents that there is much more to learning mathematics than simply completing calculations.

Not all parents wanted, or were able, to be as engaged as those described above, however. There are some parents for whom supporting the learning of their children was difficult, either because of work commitments or other caring commitments. These parents became an unseen and rather stressed presence in the background, occasionally checking on progress and asking questions but seeing the responsibility for their child's learning as the teacher's responsibility rather than a shared responsibility. Helen witnessed this first-hand as someone caring for children and older people. She was distressed by how many children and older people may have access to the technology but do not have adequate support to use it effectively. It is not a matter of simply setting things off and off we go uninterrupted. How can nations solve this inequity?

We wonder if this changed relationship between teachers and parents and carers will lead to community events in the future. It appears that there has been more openness about what teachers do and why they do it. Louise shows how the parents of her students now have access to the detail about their child's educational experience and progress. How will this transparency develop in the future?

Personal reflection on 'how the relationship with parents and community has changed'.

Chapter 8

My best 'home learning' lesson

Introduction

You have read about the challenges we all faced. The ways we all had to adapt quickly to our places of work closing down, even sometimes re-opening and then closing again. You will no doubt recognise many of these stories as they mirror your own experiences. But all the authors drew on these new experiences to plan for the future, carefully and drawing on the experience. For many of us, this new practice threw up some successes that we might not have predicted previously. The new situation allowed us to re-focus our energies and to explore how we could innovate in our planning and teaching to support remote learning. It also made us wonder how things might be different when the possibility of face-to-face teaching returned.

These new experiences are what drew us to write the book. We think that there is much to learn and to retain from what is described below. Surely, we cannot go back to teaching in the way we used to before the pandemic, when we are all back in our more usual educational settings. Surely, we can draw on what we have learnt to transform our teaching and the teaching and learning in the places in which we work.

Lucy Cooker

For my best lesson I am not going to talk about one particular session but about how we structured the online induction of the PGCEi. The one thing I am really pleased with is that we have been able to replicate small group work in the online workspace. This was really key to me. When we look at the list of aims of the induction, we did not change

DOI: 10.4324/9781003150596-8

these at all for the online version. The aims stayed the same, including getting to know your peers, which might seem challenging if you are all online. At the end of the two days students have worked in five different groups and all their feedback so far has included that they have been really pleased to get to know so many people. Along with this, colleagues who started teaching on the course soon after lockdown have said that although they did not get to know the students over two days of induction as well as they did in the previous face-to-face version, they will take advantage of the new opportunities to get to know their students through additional online meetings throughout the year. The new fully online course includes an additional three webinars for the whole cohort during the year. We have always offered individual online meetings as part of the learning on the PGCEi, but not many took up the offer. Since the first of my online webinars to introduce the requirements for the first submission I am delighted to say many more participants than before have asked for an individual meeting with me. This will allow us to explore their ideas for their first essay with me. I genuinely feel as though I am getting to know these students very well.

Tony Cotton

The information from school before I started working with Felix on his mathematics was that he was not at all confident in his abilities. His last teacher had expressed concern to his Mum and Dad, because he cried in mathematics lessons too much. I thought this response was a bit odd. If I was his teacher, I might be worrying about that and trying to do something about it rather than just telling his parents he cried too much. Anyway, during the first lockdown, Felix and I worked on lots of different areas of mathematics. Half of the time we used Cuisenaire rods which was something that was completely different to what the school did. The other half was working through some of the activities that I have written in a scheme for international schools. This meant he had a book that looked a bit like a mathematics book he would use in school. It also meant that I could convince him that we had covered content that looked like the curriculum in school. I think he enjoyed the hour every day. He enjoyed the regularity of it, and he enjoyed being successful at it. He moved from not noticing things to explaining to me how things worked and why things worked and saying, 'Oh look at that pattern!' and 'look at this!' which was great. And I think part of that was because he stopped seeing mathematics as just numbers. Or rather, he started seeing numbers as something he could do through using the Cuisenaire rods, which allowed him to see the relationships between numbers in a different way. It removed all of the previous baggage. He could do curriculum content that was quite complicated, but he was less scared of it. He started to understand that shape and space was mathematics, and that data handling was mathematics. He began to see the bigger picture. His confidence increased as a result of that and he is kind of happy giving things a go in school now he has returned and worries less about getting things wrong.

The other success was getting those participants in my online professional development sessions around the world to make contact before the session and to use the chat box. When I worked with a group in Belize, I explained that I wanted to understand where they were coming from, so I asked them to send me some photographs of the shapes that were around them to use on the presentation slides. Then I was able to use their names appearing in the sidebar, engaging them in conversation even though there were 600 in the session. Although you do not know what's happening to the other 599, it feels as though you're having a conversation with somebody. I hope for the others that felt a little bit more personal. I was interested that the feedback from the participants was that this was one of the most interactive sessions they had ever had. This shows that it is possible, through including a couple of activities expecting responses in the 'chat', to give a sense of engagement in activity.

Edward Emmet

My best lesson was definitely the 'challenges' I set every week, especially the 'taskmaster' challenge. It was not a lesson but a homework project.

The curriculum lessons that were most successful were my history lessons. We explored Queen Elizabeth I^t through songs which I learnt on drums and played for them, live and online, because they asked for it every lesson. They also loved a Bob Marley song in another live lesson. Another really effective session was a live painting lesson. I drew out and painted a scene from the Tudors and they all followed even though they did not all have paints. They wanted to learn more about Tudors, so we looked at Queen Elizabeth's speech at Tilbury. Then the children moved on to ask about Queen Victoria. It was great to go with their questions. There was never enough time, but they were really into this project. They liked using *YouTube* to research for themselves and to be interactive with me. Then they all had all the links to the clips we had looked at, so they could go back to them in their own time. Some of their parents were recapping the lessons with them and some children were choosing to do lessons time and again. This was very exciting. The girls tended to like that it was about 'princesses', but they were also into the theme of her wars as well.

Jessica Greenbaum

I remember the literature sessions. These were a genuine social experience, as we have reinstated our book clubs. Groups of children all read the same text and we discuss this text in an online meeting. This has been one of the best things this term. We have had really open, rich discussions about the books, and this leads to other areas of interest. I believe the 'Literature Groups' enabled the children to get lost in a world outside their own. Being isolated in our homes, having an 'escape' through a story that we could all 'visit' together was really profound during that time.

One of the books we read was the beautiful novel *Hitler's daughter* by Jackie French. Set in a small country town in Australia, the fictional story of Hitler's daughter Heidi is actually being told by one of the main characters to pass the time. Some of the students became intrigued by this idea, enquiring into storytelling as a pastime, whilst others were drawn down more of an historical path, enquiring into World War II and the Holocaust. For those students, some really interesting connections were made between the Germans who joined the Nazi party at the time and Trump supporters (this was during the time of the US election, and these students were trying to make sense of why certain leaders throughout history have had such a strong following).

Jasmine Irani

My best sessions were thinking of ways to be interactive and playful but still following embedding teaching targets, like 'scavenger hunts' in the house which pinpointed how they were feeling. They would find something in the house to represent how they were feeling – relating it to the 'zones of regulation'. In sessions, I might say, 'that's a cool question go and ask mum' to make it more interactive, and get the child moving around. A child who loves *Lego* and was building with it as we chatted on *Zoom*, then we had a couple of weeks of sharing songs and talking about how they felt listening to them. Also just doing very silly things over *Zoom* like playing 'Natural Disasters' where you have to act out various things such as 'Zombie Apocalypse' and 'Black Hole,' which made me laugh a lot!

Seb Jefferies

My favourite memory of online lessons was taking grammar topics that could be very dry and making them come alive. These were filmed and uploaded using *Flipgrid* (a video discussion platform). *Flipgrid* is great; it is totally secure and links to *Google classroom* with really good and straightforward editing tools.

I did a lot of work on tenses for my third graders, past, present, future. At this stage the kids had been cooped up inside and not allowed out at all. They were very bored being stuck inside. So, I created lots of scavenger hunts. I would ask the parents to hide examples of verbs in the different tenses around the house and the children would have to match the verbs in the different tenses. The parents were great and would hide them just out of reach, or make them really search hard, so that it was more fun.

For arts and crafts activities, I would upload the instructions in English, to develop the children's listening skills, or video myself doing the activity. They would carry out the activity and upload a photo or video of their final piece. This was great; I loved looking at the videos they made of their finished pieces. As I have mentioned before, some of the parents took immense care and became the filmers and editors of these final videos.

Michael Minas

I think that sending tasks home has covertly shifted the mindset of the students' family members about what mathematics is, which has been really important. I know a school that has been utilising number talks. These have been popularised by Jo Boaler and lots of detail can be found on her *Youcubed* video channel. The school sets up live chats with small groups of about six students. They thought it was important that some live teaching time was devoted to mathematics, that it should not all be dedicated to English. The idea is that number talks are inherently social. The students are socialising through discussing their strategies. These number talks also provided a more accurate assessment of what the students understood than through submitted work. You get a real sense of what children are actually thinking and teachers can also be confident that there has not been any parental intervention, which is not the case when assessing submitted work completed at home. Number talks also gave their teachers a better sense of what they should do next to follow up the learning. There were some great sessions where children would solve mathematics problems live and share their strategies on a *padlet*. Some children were great at taking photographs of their solutions too, which helped with the challenges of trying to represent their thinking accurately via a keyboard.

Amanda Queiroz Moura

I have some students with special needs. I come from an academic background of studying mathematics and inclusion. Part of my commitment to inclusion is to talk to each of my students and ask, 'What can I improve in my classes?' Based on their responses I prepare different activities, especially the assessments. We have a big assessment, 60% of your curriculum assessment depends on your score in this test. So, I use examples about a football team, or one lesson has Katy Perry (a famous singer) as a topic. This works. They score well on the test and write emails to thank me because of my approach.

I do not have the chance to innovate too much because of the tests, but I started to share my screen using the online platform and to share my writing. When I started to use this method, we started to have good experiences. In the first trimester I have students who do not work well in mathematics; they do not even get a minimal score. They were very upset, and I talked to them and explained how you go back over the class of the week and try to resolve your mistakes and the students started to change. I said, 'I believe in you; it's a hard time for everyone'. So, although they have anxiety and uncertainly about the future, they have changed and participated. Now, in the second trimester they have a good score. I think the difference was the dialogue. I was on their side, not against them; I opened a space for them to talk to me about their anxieties and life. It is the way I'm trying to resolve these things with them. I will ask, 'What happened, you do not deliver the homework in the time?' I am trying this personal approach. Trying to show them they are special to me. I have built the relationship slowly online.

It is a new way to teach so we can compare. It seems very slow. The answers are not fast. You need more time. I am learning and realising the difficulties of the teachers. When we are in the room we can see if the students are engaged or not. Then we can invent different tasks for the students. I have grown to really like the investigation methodology, creating new activities, games in their rooms at home.

Nicodemus Amboko Muhati

Around May 2020 I was teaching about the League of Nations and I remember my students were really excited when Kenya was mentioned as a member of the Security Council. Now they told me they want to take full charge of the learning because in my class there is democracy. I have embraced democracy very well, being a teacher of history. Democracy is a concept that we teach widely in history, so one of the things that I try to implement in my classroom is democracy, that is, democracy where students speak and take charge of the learning. They also take charge of the assessment and can express themselves the way they want. That gives me an opportunity as a teacher to guide them appropriately. So, my students took charge of their own learning and research. They looked at the failures of the League of Nations and did a comparative analysis with the United Nations of today. They did a lot of research. They did a lot of reading. They interviewed parents with connections to the United Nations. They came to class with videos recorded and were excited about it. I just could not figure out how this was happening.

Initially, I had been a bit sceptical. What will happen? Now my kids can speak like the real ambassadors of the United Nations and that really makes me so happy. I was in class, not as a custodian of knowledge but as a facilitator of learning, because the kids did the projects themselves. When you give children an opportunity to say what they are able to, it motivates them so much. But when you say, 'No, this is what I want you to do. I have prepared my PowerPoint and now we have to do this'. The next time you meet these children in class, they do not have that motivation to continue learning. Student-centred pedagogy was actualised during that teaching learning moment and, until today, I think it is one of the best teaching moments I have ever had.

Betty Sheila Mumbi

First of all, I think just the ability of students to be sat at a computer and complete their lessons on a daily basis is a success in itself. And seeing them improve from maybe where we started in the first week of the term and where we have got to is also another one. Another success is seeing the students be able to lead other students as well and take charge, assist other students who may be struggling with technology. Well, just understanding has also been a success. And when they send in recordings with evidence of them doing different things at home and taking part in, say, cooking at home, or cleaning, it is a success as well. They have gained several things from this process, such as responsibility and leadership. They have grown quite a lot. I think this pandemic makes you grow in ways you did not think you could. It shifts your mind to a lot of things to make you a bit stronger, mentally.

Hubert Mathanzima Mweli

The pandemic has indeed taught us to do things differently. For the education system as big as ours, which has nine provincial education departments and 74 education districts over and above the National Department of Education, to meet almost every week to put plans together was the greatest lesson. We have been able to produce great work that saved the academic year at the 'online working space'. The resourcefulness of this privilege continues within the sector and planning and oversight could not be easier.

Helen Toft

A student in China, who had moved house after lockdown, had been struggling with the academic demands of the PGCEi course as well as where she was living. She seemed very different once she had moved apartment. She was more relaxed and open and feeling a little more confident about her studies. She started asking questions about the features of the room. I showed her round the rest of the room briefly and she was entranced. She said she was inspired to decorate her house in a similar way.

Although this possible 'intrusiveness' might not suit some teaching situations I have found that sharing spaces has deepened connections. This episode led to a great tutorial where she was articulating her reading really insightfully. Her six-year-old daughter joined in and the student remained calm and focused. She has since submitted a brilliant essay. We had never had such a relaxed tutorial and it felt like the personalisation, the way we shared the places in which we felt safe and happy, meant we put things into context for her thinking and writing about education.

A similar event happened with choir. We have deepened our commitment to the whole choir by looking after one another. We sometimes share something of our homes with each other to develop the bond of singing that our love of Thanda, as a leader and a human being, has given us. This would never have happened pre-pandemic.

Delmer Tzib

My discussion around the 'banana republics'. There is already excellent material online in terms of videos that I could download. There is lots of good material on *YouTube*. There is a wealth of readings, mainly academic papers, that I could extract notes from for the students. I would rewrite these papers so that they were suitable for them.

I used a series of cartoons, political cartoons. They created their own cartoons. I wanted to know what they were thinking as well as what they were understanding. I don't want them to just remember the dates; I want them to understand the significance of what happened on those dates and to ask why something happened not when it happened.

Louise Whyte

I would say my best lesson was with Year 12. Our school does not subscribe to scientific journals, but I think they are important for enriching A-level and because students were at home with their own devices, it was just a case of showing them where they can get the information via open access. Some decided to work on their own and some in groups of three or four, reading several different articles, summarising them, and then choosing which platform to use to present their findings, which resulted in some amazing interactive presentations, games and videos. In sixth form here they do not get much time to do this type of learning. Previously, we had talked about the value of peer review with a few examples, but it is only when they went away and read 10–12 articles themselves that they started to understand the value of the scientific method.

As a department we discussed how we could incorporate more practical activities for younger students and one very successful scheme we developed involved giving students a list of household objects that related to what we were studying, and a list of key facts and theories and students had to match and link them into a presentation using the platform of their choice. During the lessons they were up and about and then coming back to the screen. Previously we had had problems with students not wanting to be on screen, but when they had to go and collect something and show it, they were a lot happier with also showing themselves. A couple of times, we even had a grandmother get involved, showing her electric hair curlers for an energy transfer unit! As staff we needed that interaction; we had begun to feel quite lonely teaching classes without cameras on and it was clear that students gained a lot from these more engaging lessons.

Vicky Van Wyk

I really enjoyed scavenger hunts with the younger children. They had so much fun having to look for something at home and running against the clock to find an object to show in class. For example, the colour green. I loved this lesson and it created such a positive atmosphere in class. The children had five minutes, timed, to find as many green things as they could around the apartment. They would run off, run around, and bring back plants, a shoe or broccoli (say). It was amazing what they came up with. It was definitely an interesting lesson because in class they would preview what their peers would bring to school and either bring the same object or try to bring something better.

During this lesson there wasn't much of a choice as they couldn't compare beforehand and had to make do with what they had.

I would surround my lesson around vocabulary through a show and tell, descriptions, colours and uses of the object. For example:

- Where did you find it? (Link to a large or small area, which would link to sizes and mathematics)
- Is it a fruit, a vegetable? (Link to Science and where this food can grow, what it needs to grow)
- Do you like it? (Linking to their personal opinion and furthering their vocabulary on their thought process)

We would discuss everyone's object, one at a time, and everyone would have the chance to chime in with their opinions. It was a wonderful lesson.

Reflections

This is another chapter which had an immediate impact on our teaching. As we read each other's stories we could immediately draw inspiration for our own teaching. We hope that readers of this book will develop and change their teaching as a result of engaging with these stories. We are fairly certain that this will happen because it has happened for all the authors!

We know that people can form relationships online. We may know people who are in loving relationships having met 'online'. We also know how important safeguarding our learners is too. More evidence of the power of the internet to develop relationships. Many of these examples show how the platforms for online learning can be effectively used for groupwork. And, that through this groupwork learners can create and develop a community of learners. Tony describes how the Belize teachers felt actively engaged through communicating with each other using the chat bar; Jess recreated a 'book group' with her younger learners and Louise set her students up as scientific researchers exploring the world of scientific journals.

These relationships also developed at an individual level. Perhaps online learning offers us the chance to personalise the learning journey more. Helen describes how one of her students felt more able to rise to the challenge of academic writing after sharing their homes through an online 'tour'. Amanda describes how the hard work of keeping dialogue open at an individual level paid off in terms of learning. Mr Muhati wonders if online learning offers a more democratic way of learning and is supported by Betty, who suggests, 'Students speak and take charge of the learning'. She describes how this more democratic approach meant that students gained responsibility and leadership. Important lessons for life.

One thing that is immediately noticeable is that our favourite moments all involved ensuring that the learning was active. Maybe a surprise as online learning may be perceived as passive. There are many examples of using the possibilities of the internet for research and multimedia approaches, including games and videos. Jasmine shares the ways she engaged the children she works with and Seb and Vicky have both enjoyed scavenger hunts. Tony and Helen can confirm the success of scavenger hunts as these are now a regular part of home schooling their grandsons. The placing of the power in the hands of the learner, whether the learner is three or 93, has also offered the potential for deepening learning because sessions can be recorded and revisited. Images can be magnified and studied close-up whilst researching for an art project, for example.

The previous chapter discussed ways in which parents and carers could be involved in home schooling. One of the ways we measured the success of our best sessions was the extent to which parent's views of the nature of the subject and the reasons underpinning the pedagogical approach we were taking could be altered through the process. Michael describes how he has changed parent's views of mathematics through their involvement in online learning.

Finally, and perhaps most radically, working online has forced us to slow learning down. It snaps us out of the conveyor belt view of teaching and learning in which students are on a belt and move round teachers and exercise without any time for reflection. Seb describes how the whole family would enjoy the craft sessions which he would introduce and that would be completed over time and then recording the outcomes and sharing them through uploading them to the secure platform used by the school. This reminds us that learning takes place over time, not instantaneously. As Amanda states, 'I have really grown to like the investigation methodology'.

These stories have shifted our thinking around planning for online learning. We now have a checklist we can use to audit our planning. We can ask ourselves,

To what extent does our online learning session:

- Allow for group work and support learners developing positive relationships in their group?
- Allow for personalisation of learning?
- Expect learners to be active?
- Set challenges which will be reported back on later?
- Involve parents, carers or other adults?
- Slow learning down?

> **What was the best lesson that you taught during periods of online teaching and learning? Did it share any elements with the lessons above?**

Chapter 9

What have we learned from teaching under the pandemic?

Introduction

They say that we learn very quickly at times of crisis. This certainly seems to be the case for this group of educators. You read in the last chapter about the ways the authors found to engage their learners using online platforms. You also read about how the authors tried to replicate those practices that were important to them when working face to face and about how we all came to realise that there are actually some ways of learning and teaching that are more effective virtually.

Perhaps the change in the situation, with so many of us working and teaching from home, working in isolation from others, meant that we found time and space to reflect on what we were learning about learning and teaching in general.

Lucy Cooker

I think there are four main areas where I think that I have learned things about myself and about learning and teaching. I think the way that I worked online and collaboratively with university colleagues has shown that I am able to take a leadership role and I am really proud of 'holding' my colleagues together when they were worried. This has given me confidence as I move into the new leadership role I have taken on.

My experience in writing this book has taught me that whilst it was lovely to meet physically on occasions, the meetings to put the book together could work just as well online. This may be because we know each other so well, from working together and from writing *Being a teacher*. Meeting virtually also saves an awful lot of travelling time!

My focus in my new role has been sorting out all the issues with technology and administrative details. This has made me wonder if it

DOI: 10.4324/9781003150596-9

has been good for me not to know too much about other day-to-day course details for the PGCEi, which was the course I was most attached to previously. I should be pulling out of the role of leading the PGCEi now to leave space for the new course leader to take control and ownership of the course.

Although everyone that has previously taught on the PGCEi would love to see the face-to-face induction come back and knows that there is something about travel and having a shared experience in a new country that is hard to replicate, we also know that we can run the induction programme online. This has been a powerful learning experience.

Tony Cotton

I think it is about noticing what happens. It is about not being too scared about getting it right the first time because you do not know what getting it right looks like or feels like till you have tried some things out. So not worrying about that. Not trying to simply replicate what has gone before, but think, okay what do we want at the end of this? What equipment, what new tools have we got to get there? How might that resource get us to that endpoint? And I think just learning from many other people in a whole range of different contexts. This is something that I have always tried to do anyway. I guess this is mainly because I am incredibly lucky enough to work with lots of different educators in lots of different countries.

I talked about opening up the chat box before each session and welcoming people into the session through some informal conversations. Even though there were 600 in the group, this solved the problem of online teaching or webinars feeling very impersonal. I think I said earlier that this came from a musician friend of mine doing an online gig. We were trying to solve the same problem. How do we create some kind of an intimacy so that people are or feel involved, so that they are a presence and an energy in the room? I saw him solve this problem by saying, 'Hi, great that you could come Helen'. Even though we were all watching the gig in our own homes it suddenly felt like we were all in the same space.

I think what we do not know is who is going to gain and who is going to lose from this new way of working. We have to take care to notice that. There will be new problems to solve depending on what we notice. We will be including people now that we were not including before. We will be excluding people now that we were not excluding before. And we have to try and notice how that has shifted and think what we have to do differently as a result. In South Africa and Belize, they use community and national radio for learning at home. This is because people have not got access to the internet at all. They have also been using *WhatsApp* because most people have got a mobile phone. So, we need to make sure we work out how best to use *WhatsApp* and things like that and not just the fancy and flashy platforms that are being developed. I think we are just starting to work out how this stuff works.

Edward Emmet

I think that we were under such intense pressure that I did not sort problems out very well. Looking back, I think I should have had a more flexible approach. My internet sometimes did not connect, and I was at home trying really hard to sort things out, but the parents put us under real pressure to solve problems very quickly. Children would 'freeze' because of internet problems during lessons. This meant that I was always teaching with my fingers crossed every lesson. I felt quite anxious about parents and children if they were not learning because I felt so much pressure to cover the full curriculum. That was never really resolved.

Jessica Greenbaum

I think the most important lesson is the involvement of families in learning. That we should make early contact with families explaining both what we do and what we teach and why we do it in the way we do. This links to the importance of relationships in education. Relationships between teachers; between teachers and learners; and between teachers and parents and the community. We need to explore how we can continue to develop and support these relationships in online learning. I have certainly been reminded of the value of working in a team and working collaboratively.

Prior to moving to remote teaching and learning, teaching teams (made up of the teachers within the same year level) would plan the overarching unit planners together but then carry out those broad plans individually in separate classrooms behind closed doors. We acknowledge and celebrate the fact that we all bring a different 'flavour' to our teaching style. It was during remote teaching, however, that we were able to really observe those individual differences and learn from them. As we had a joint *Google Classroom* for the entire Year 3/4 cohort, everything was shared. We divided the learning areas (Reading, Writing, Maths and Inquiry) and worked in pairs on one or two of those subjects for a few weeks, then rotated both the subject and the planning partner. It was almost like an ongoing peer-observation programme. At the end of each week, as we prepared for the following, we reviewed the plans and associated tasks/instructional videos of the others. We offered and received constructive feedback and made the suggested changes before sending it out to the students.

Transitioning back to onsite learning, we tried to continue with this approach but found it was too time consuming and at times too prescriptive as it didn't respond to the individual needs within one's own classroom (something that was more challenging to do during remote learning).

Jasmine Irani

Most interesting was that *Zoom* made learning more accessible to some of our kids. Coming to an after-school session is a really big deal; parents struggle to get them to come. At home they just had to log on; the parent was there somewhere, but they might be in their bedroom, and they could 'mute' themselves or turn the video off. The choices they had were making it possible to access something they do not find easy; sensory issues are really not easy to cope with. A good host can mute or can control the loudness. In face-to-face sessions this can become very challenging. *Zoom* options definitely made our sessions more accessible. Also, it was brilliant because although we are based in Brighton and London, we could have someone from Preston join us and we worked with a Canadian colleague. This made it a novel way to work.

Lots of the children had things to show, *Lego* models and the like, and I was growing seeds, giving updates on the sunflowers I was growing. All the children got to know each other more and more; the adults were leaving them to chat amongst themselves, letting them hang out together and this helped them to develop more independent social skills.

Seb Jefferies

I think that the children have had the freedom to make choices about when they do things and what order they do things in. They all have different waking hours and sleeping patterns, so the virtual platforms have given them the freedom to do things in their own time. This is an important piece of learning for me when I think about what happens in classrooms. I need to work out how I can give children some of this freedom back in the classroom.

I hope that in the future homework could become something exciting and creative. I can use the apps in the same way as I did when teaching remotely so that homework becomes much more active and engaging. I can use the video resources I have created for this homework. Perhaps an example would be that the children can then send me videos of themselves speaking English which I can 'mark' later in the evening.

It has been interesting that one of the things they have loved doing is sending me videos of themselves reading poetry. They really like reading poetry to me. This is part of the culture too. Being a poet in Mongolia is a legitimate profession. This is something I need to build into my teaching more once we are back in school.

Michael Minas

Some styles of lessons lend themselves to being recorded and stored digitally, for example, a strategies approach to learning multiplication facts. A teacher could record a series of short videos, which students could then access when they need them.

Amanda Queiroz Moura

Definitively another experience with online classes will be less stressful. I discovered that my problems were more related to the choices of the school than to me or my methods, or even with the whole idea of online classes. At the college, I taught a different course with new students; they also did not open the camera; however, we got to construct a great relationship as I was freer concerning the methods of teaching. I could create more dynamic classes that incentivised the participation of the students. Certainly, these were pleasant classes for me and for the students.

Nicodemus Amboko Muhati

One of the biggest takeaways from this experience of remote teaching and learning goes back to what my tutor told me during my PGCEi – flexibility. You have to be flexible. Another thing, as a classroom practitioner I have to always believe that something is possible. It can be done, and it will be done! I believe in possibilities, so if you have a very positive attitude as a classroom practitioner, it is just a matter of trying to be flexible. Try to consult. Even, maybe especially, the students will give you ideas which you can develop. So, flexibility is my biggest takeaway.

Betty Sheila Mumbi

You need to think outside the box. For example, when the connection in your house goes off or power goes out and you are in the middle of a lesson, you do need to think quickly about how students can still engage and get back into the lesson. One time last week both my colleague and I were in a meeting with about 12 students and we were in different places in different sides of the school and I did not realise it. The power went out and the internet went down as well. I was not in my house, so I tried to run to my house, because I thought maybe something had happened there. And just as I got to my house, my colleague called me on the phone to say he did not have internet either and asked me if I was still on the call. And I said, 'No, I've been kicked out of the call', so we both pretty much went into a panic now because there are a group of students on the call alone, and because we have both been kicked out of the call. So, at that point I purchased time on the internet on my phone, then reconnected back into the lesson and carried on with the lesson. Yes, that was a hectic one.

There have been a lot of things we have had to learn as we go. I do not think anyone ever saw this happening, so it is something that the whole world is learning to do as we go. Taking each day as it comes.

Hubert Mathanzima Mweli

What the pandemic has brought to the fore is how low and unequally distributed the skills and availability of resources are in relation to the use of digital learning materials. Many of South Africa's teachers access too little of their own professional development materials online. We are even behind Vietnam and Brazil in this regard, according to the 2017 Teaching and Learning International Survey (TALIS). The Department of Basic Education has worked hard on improving the supply of digital learning materials aimed at both learners and educators. I believe the educator side could receive even more attention, and that this should be linked to current initiatives on promoting teacher centres and locally driven professional learning communities (PLCs). It is only by making teachers enthusiastic and knowledgeable about remote learning and digital materials aimed at themselves that they will become effective promoters of a more modern and digitally focused mode of learning among their learners. A more digitally in-tune sector, especially as far as disadvantaged schools are concerned, is a sector that will be more resilient to future shocks of the kind that have hit us in 2020.

Helen Toft

The struggles with the technology in the choir and with our grandchildren taught me so much. At one stage some members of the choir wondered whether to carry on as it had been so challenging for weeks. I think the resolution of this came not from mastery of the IT, although there have been huge strides with this recently, leading to very satisfying outcomes. I believe it was the Black Lives Matter talk Thanda inspired us with, and we realised we had so much to learn and that we were a surprising source of strength for him. He has also drawn on the many other teaching and learning experiences he was engaged in virtually and applies them to our choir with energy and delight. Now it has become second nature to record things to share later, muting, sharing his screen and so on, all the usual virtual meeting protocols, but it was the emotional connection which inspired us all to dig deep and commit. Late February lessons have included examples of members sharing real insight and knowledge of their favourite solos; 'our' songs inspiring Thanda in his work with the 'Opera North' young people's choir and long-forgotten harmonies surfacing beautifully.

Working with Felix, Thanda confidently starts from where the child wants to start rather than trying to impose a lesson plan on the session, and screen sharing can have a deep impact on both the eight and three-year-old with song and stories.

My sadness at losing the face-to-face element of the PGCEi was overcome by actually running a virtual induction. I had months of concern that I would not be able to make a good enough connection with the students if we were not being actively creative together in a classroom, but Tony and I worked on this together and found ways. For example, before the main induction session we run a tech test to check that all the students can access the platform that the training will take place on and that their technology is working. Rather than just turn cameras on and off as a test we asked all the students to bring and share an item which was of importance and significance to them. This activity built a sense of community even though we were all sitting in separate spaces all around the world. I took notes (yes, pen and paper!) and shared the following poem with the group as a reminder of this. Some students said this activity was important.

> *A piece of silver to celebrate a child's birth, a cuddly giraffe or a ring chosen by your young children 'all by themselves'*
> *a silver acorn of knowledge and wisdom*
> *a model of a 'honeypot' flower, a beautifully beaded giraffe from your home country*
> *a pipe to remind you of the Highland pipes played back home*
> *a fridge magnet of architecture in your adopted country*
> *a note from a dear friend on a used boarding pass or a postcard with 'keep holding on' to help with the homesickness*
> *a favourite novel with its English translation*
> *a handmade thank you card from a colleague or a much loved home knitted sock*
> *an electronic book reader, a 'physical' favourite travel guide, a Cassio calculator or a well-loved wallet reminding of loved ones which go everywhere with you*
> *or a journal of thankfulness meditations*
> *unpacked boxes from the most recent house move*
> *a so necessary whiteboard pen*
> *and of course in the new Covid era, a bottle of sanitiser...and more –*
> *the same things matter to us all no matter where we live, work, study or find ourselves in the world. We need our friends, family and colleagues to support us; creative, intellectual and mindful tools, challenge and satisfaction; treasured mementos and of course the ability to keep virus free. If we live in*
> *Egypt, Thailand, Uruguay, Russia, Singapore or were from South Africa, Namibia, England, Scotland, the US, Spain, Siberia and beyond so much of our lives as educators connect.*

Another way of feeling 'present' at the virtual event was to make sure, even though we were not officially required to do so, that we were actually present at the computer when sessions started and finished. This did mean that we had to get up at 3 am due to time differences, but Tony and I pretended the tiredness was the jet lag we normally experience when travelling to Bangkok and working. We also tried to replicate the ways that we would reflect on sessions as soon as they finished by visiting coffee shops (which were open at this stage) early in the morning – it felt more like a 'normal' workday on induction, and we reflected excitedly, just as we do in Bangkok.

Finally, the ability to attend a big meeting, 100+ attendees, led, in my case, by five black academics from around the UK, who spoke so candidly of their experiences, hopes and fears for the future of higher education and their place in it was a defining moment. Hearing the impact, not just of the 'BLM movement', but of lives lived under oppression in South Africa from Thanda and the UK from Thanda and the academics on my screen, in my home office, made the consequences inescapable for us all, as they should be.

Delmer Tzib

Education is a way to freedom. To the freedom of the mind and the only way we can move towards this is to focus on analytical and critical thinking; focus on asking questions and finding answers to these questions.

I think teachers have discovered that they can be easily replaced by the internet. If they are just repositories of facts that students can find out these facts more simply by searching the net. I have to be much more than someone who just stands in for a dictionary or a book. I think this can empower students to think for themselves.

I think students are very astute. They talk to each other and communicate very well, but many are not open to having critical thinking in the classroom. But the focus on analysis helps to break these ideas that some students may have of finding ways around their challenges. That strategy has worked for me because they are engaged not with only facts but ideas that they need to evaluate and think about. They experience, reflect and are encouraged to think in order to act.

Louise Whyte

For me it was about making the time to trial everything. We received a lot of links to websites and instructions to try this and try that, and initially it was quite overwhelming. I had to be very creative and take full responsibility for my own professional development. Some of the resources and programmes have transformed my teaching and some have solved problems that I didn't necessarily know I had. Teachers and students are regularly implementing practices used during online learning now we are back in the physical classroom.

There are so many resources that have been put out there in the last two or three years that it's just phenomenal. It's about trying to keep making time to use them and critically evaluate them to see if they really do work for the students. We did discover that the students' IT skills were quite poor, they needed to be guided through how to access and use the resources in much more detail than I had anticipated.

Vicky Van Wyck

I think we need to find more ways to really have fun in class. Maybe have one theme and create many different activities around it. Instead of expecting so much of children because the curriculum expects it or because the school expects it, we should focus on the children's needs and well-being. The school, the curriculum, the textbook does not understand what these children are experiencing at this given time during the pandemic. They need to learn through means of play and further develop their sensorial skills. We need to find more interactive ways to do this online. I thought it would be a good idea to send home 'care packages' for children which they can make use of during class, or even after class when they might become a bit bored. These packages would include resources like play doh, scrap paper, glitter sticks, clay and modelling materials so these students can have access to some sensorial resources to get their creative juices flowing.

Reflections

It seems fairly obvious, but we all learned, very quickly, about the technology and for many of us this was new technology. Whilst we all have used computers in the past, the platforms we were using for teaching were very new to most of us. We had to explore the features and decide which ones could replicate or improve on the ways of working we may have used in a physical classroom. We also explored new ways of working which were only possible with the new technology and used the technology to its strengths. For example, writing this book took a new form; we wrote it in less than a year rather than over three years largely as a result of becoming comfortable with meeting virtually. This saved a lot of time in travelling within the UK and also meant we could fairly quicky set up interviews with the global writing team and share the outcomes. But, there were times when it was important to meet. When we hit a couple of challenges, we all needed to sit in the same room to give each other support and confidence.

There are several instances of how it is becoming quite usual to record sessions. This means people can access training, such as that provided by Tony or Michael at any time. This opens up access. Those colleagues who may not be able to join live sessions can access them when their lives allow. Delmer and Amanda have previously mentioned how useful their students found it to be able to revisit presentations to explore challenging areas again. This may also be helpful in terms of working in partnership with those that are supporting our learners. The question 'How did the teacher explain it?' becomes easier to explain when the evidence is online.

Using technology to involve parents is an area that Jess has found helpful and it feels like we need to make sure we continue this genuine form of educating as a partnership. Other partnerships that are only possible through using technology include the panels involving black academics that were so important to Helen. We have realised that it has become possible to set up genuinely diverse panels or specialist panels with global experience without too much difficulty. In fact, the challenge becomes networking so that we become aware of the skills we can draw on from all around the world. We can genuinely see the world as providing the teachers in our schools. Jasmine shows us how when she describes involving colleagues from around the UK and Canada.

A thread that has wound its way through this book is how technology can be used to hand over control to our learners. If we allow it and move away from the idea of synchronous teaching as the predominant mode of online teaching and learning, then learners can take control over where and when they engage with activities. Technology also gives them opportunities to share the outcomes of their learning in different ways. This is what Delmer sees as education being the way to freedom. The chat function has become key to sharing ideas during the sessions and an important form of feedback at the end of sessions. Maybe this is something we can all build into future practice, gaining immediate feedback from our learners by asking them to post a sentence which summarises the key ideas they are taking away from the session.

We have been reminded about the inequity that exists in education. As we moved to online teaching and learning this inequity showed itself particularly in terms of access to resources that support learning. Hubert Mweli reminds us of this at a national level and we know it is the case at an international level. This is an important structural issue that needs to be prioritised and sorted at a governmental and even global level. If learning is to be transformed as a result of what we have learned since the pandemic hit, and that hope drives this book, then we need to ensure access to new ways of learning is distributed more fairly. We can already see the inequities that are built into the system as the vaccine is rolled out much more quickly in richer areas of the world.

Another area in which the new ways of working could support a more equitable and socially just education system is through noticing what the impact of new ways of learning is having on learners. We can notice the impact on our learners to make sure new ways of learning do support inclusivity. For example, *Zoom* makes sessions more accessible for some of the learners that Jasmine works with, particularly those who find being in school challenging.

Many of the stories show how much we have learned about ourselves. The speed with which we had to respond have shown us skills we did not know we had and pointed to areas which we needed to develop very quickly! The way in which we responded also made transparent our values and beliefs. We had to focus quickly on what we felt was important in education and try to make sure that drove the innovations. What skills have we seen as important over the last 18 months or so. Edward, Mr Muhati and others suggest we need to make sure we can respond flexibly, something that was made difficult by those running schools or education at a national level who imposed ways of working quickly without thinking through the implications, or consulting with those that know best – the educators themselves. One of the things we need to allow ourselves going forward is to remember it is okay to take risks. This will allow us to think outside the box, as recommended by Betty, and to give ourselves to trial everything, which Louise sees as vital.

Finally, we must not forget that we need to find ways to have fun in the classroom, virtual or otherwise. Thank you, Vicky, for making sure this is at the top of any list of best lessons.

What is the best lesson you taught online? How was it similar and how was it different to the lessons and activities described above?

Part 3

Looking to the future

Chapter 10

Innovations that will persist

Introduction

So, how might our teaching be transformed as a result of the changes that the pandemic has forced on us? What have we realised are the practices that should stay with us? What have we come to realise about learning that makes us question our previous, maybe taken-for-granted pedagogical approaches? Here are the transformations and innovations that this particular group of educators think should endure.

Lucy Cooker

We could and should always have a wholly online induction for those who cannot afford or take the time. This cohort would be a lovely diverse cohort from *anywhere* in the world. Attending face-to-face sessions ratchets up the demands on a student more, and there are all those issues about social inclusion I talked about before. If we did go back to the face-to-face induction sessions, I think what we would take with us from the online induction is quite significant. Colleagues who could not or did not want to fly could be accommodated. And, we must consider the environment. The banning of all travel by the university has had a massive impact on reducing travel, accommodation and even the amount of photocopying we used to do, not just on our course but throughout the university. We reduce the environmental impact of the whole education industry with this innovation.

Finally, in all of my roles, there is something really lovely in being able to connect instantly with anyone anywhere in the world for any task or meeting. I think there has been a kind of emotional resistance

DOI: 10.4324/9781003150596-10

to online working from all of us. But, it is so much easier to carry on developing a new version of the course when you have the basics that existed already. This is a massive gain. You never know, maybe the thought of getting on a plane to go to work in the future will just be so tedious (lots of laughter).

Tony Cotton

I am not going to be going to lots of meetings anymore. I shall certainly use *Zoom* and *Teams* for many of my meetings. I do think there is something in it being a mixture of online and live, and I think getting that mixture right is going to be important. We need to make sure we continue teaching and learning online for the right reasons rather than just doing it for economic reasons. There is something about the flexibility in the adaptability of the technology, which is helpful and supportive and exciting. But there is also that immediacy and dynamism, which is lost in the online sessions that is so hard to replicate compared to face to face.

I think it is hard to know what will persist. We are only just seeing what is possible. Can I use an example from outside education to explain what I mean? Before the pandemic I used to go to watch Bradford City with two friends and my brother. We all have season tickets and every two weeks would spend the afternoon together. For me going 'to the match' was very much a communal and community experience. There have been no crowds at football matches for nearly a year now but we are able to watch every game on the internet. So, we have changed our ritual. We set up a *WhatsApp* group, watch the game in our own homes, on our own screens and replicate the inane but very important discussions about the game's progress on *WhatsApp*. This is now a weekly and often twice-weekly event as we can 'attend' away games without travelling. I can imagine that in the future 'having a season ticket' may include access to the event online as an option and that physical attendance may be a choice we could make, particularly when we are able to sit together in one of our houses.

What might this look like in school? Perhaps lessons may take a different form. Students may be expected to spend considerable amounts of time in an individual learning space preparing for their time with a teacher. Teaching groups could be halved with half a group engaged in self-study whilst the teacher has tutorial time with the other students. I think blended learning could become a norm.

Edward Emmet

We went back to school in June, but things have really changed. Parents are no longer allowed on campus; usually everyone is on site and we lost teaching time. Now we have to take the children to and from a drop-off point; their name is called, and we almost throw them into the car. The head has said it works so well that we will keep this as a normal routine, but there is consequently much less communication with the parents. There is an upside as arrival and home time are more organised; parents were not picking up children on time before, which I did not think of as an issue as I liked the children playing in my room while I got ready, but now we are going through an accreditation process as an International Baccalaureate (IB) school, so we do have more time to work.

As I said before, the one thing I have focused on during lockdown was promoting reading as much as possible due to the benefits for all children in all subject areas. My current class, who moved up to me after lockdown and had not had any schooling, are at so much lower levels than expected, so we are doing a lot of kindergarten work still. I do not want to complain to their teachers; I have to be diplomatic and they did not teach these reception children online. Still, the parents are asking why their child is not reading so well because I am asking them to 'Please read over half term a lot with your child'.

Everything is more or less back to normal though we are still social distancing. We are not supposed to be working in groups, but the children do really. Lunch times are staggered to avoid crowds which makes the timetable a mess; our lunch is at 11.30, then it is 'topic' and suddenly time to pack bags for home time. I think we need to build much more flexibility in the curriculum to cope with the physical changes. I continue to video homework tasks, say a five-minute music class, and post this on a chat. Just one more point, I had a wonderful session when my dad (who I wrote about in the last book) recorded a 'Stay at Home' song for his early years' children in south London, and my kids in Thailand loved learning this song in English. This is something which would never have happened without lockdown. In some ways this shared crisis has brought us closer together.

Jessica Greenbaum

We need to continue to consider everybody's role in education, particularly parents as partners in education. Children need stimulation from parents as well as from teachers. One of the questions that we all need to ask ourselves is 'How do we engage with our community to convince them that they are partners in their children's learning'.

The use of technology, *Google classroom*, for example, the idea of kids submitting their work through *Google classroom* means I can give individual feedback using the technology and this makes the teaching more personal. Filming lessons makes us more concise. It has made us more thoughtful about what we are saying; made us think about what we are doing. If we know that parents might be watching the video we will think carefully about what we present to the learners.

Jasmine Irani

Going forward one group is carrying on as a *Zoom* meeting. The school they used to meet in does not want kids from ten different schools coming together in their school because of the risk of virus spreading. We run another group in a library and another in a children's centre. We probably need to find somewhere like this for the school-based group eventually.

Another unexpected positive was that daytime groups for home-schooled children are expensive of our professional time, but over *Zoom* it is a lot cheaper. Travelling time is expensive, so more activity is feasible in a day if we plan well; working using online platforms uses our time better. We are learning to manage this so that we can collaborate with other professionals. For example, a speech and language assessment was going on face to face with a therapist the other day but I used *Zoom* to join in for a while.

One little boy responded better on screen than he did in face-to-face sessions. He loved PowerPoint treasure hunts using his favourite characters, so we are going to continue using these scripts to develop his skills when face to face. For example, we were working on his food tolerance with his mum sitting with him; the therapist was asking, 'Can you touch it? Can you lick it?' and mum was doing it next to him. Having the visuals as well as us on *Zoom* and his mum in the room was helping. All his workers can use the same PowerPoint with him.

Social distancing is not good for those who find social interaction challenging. But not having the pressure of being in school, which is a cause of real anxiety for many of these children, helped. Being at home is calmer. This seems to have helped learning. But socially is where lockdown has made it trickier. Our work is based on the need to develop social skills; that is why the child has the diagnosis. What could happen is that they practised with family face to face and with us over *Zoom*, so they were taking first slower steps to develop those skills, social signifiers like telling a joke or sharing news about toys. Moving on to being with other children and their peers after they have had time to practise before going into the more complex social setting. I am working with one child to get them ready to go back into school. I work with them on recognising their emotions, recognising when they need to calm down, asking for breaks. It has been great being able to simplify things, put things into place proactively, before they go into school. This means we might be able to pre-empt an issue.

I was so proud because the kids were so resilient; everyone was having a hard time. Social skills group made me laugh with their 'good news' for the week or someone saying something really kind to another. I have also noticed that because there were fewer distractions using online platforms I noticed more things than I used to. My focus was all on one screen, so I could not miss anything; the online platform made it easier to notice things. I need to find ways to maintain this focus in our face-to-face sessions.

Going back to face to face was so nice – going into homes there was obviously anxiety about safety, but it's so nice to be able to actually play. I think now, though we will be more flexible with our options and what works, everyone is so individual it's beneficial to see how we can teach from a whole bank of new ways of working.

Seb Jefferies

Well, we are already back in school and the social distancing rules have made the classroom less active, which is challenging for me. Currently, we are not allowed to give homework, which I agree with as the working day for some students does not finish until 6.00 pm. I hope that when we are through the pandemic I will be able to allow students to choose to send me their 'work' online or bring it to class. I hope that there will be increased student choice and freedom for the children to have a voice in how and what they want to learn.

My students have been really inspiring throughout the pandemic – this has made me up my game.

Amanda Queiroz Moura

I feel that it will be difficult to forget these online experiences. I imagine we will bring a lot of things to face-to-face classes. But my big challenge in the next month is that I will be back in the classroom and I will need to fit into the new school. I work in traditional schools, so I suggested a topic, but they said, 'You must continue with exercises to solve problems'. They maintain the same style of traditional classes and I cannot invent new things like I did in online classes. I have a doubt about this book, the Brazilian reality is special, how will it appear to the world? My students are privileged, but most of the children do not have the chance to have lessons during the pandemic; the teachers didn't have a chance to teach them properly.

Nicodemus Amboko Muhati

I do not see remote teaching and learning (RTL) going away. I think RTL is now here to stay. I know many parents who have decided to withdraw their children from this schooling system and begin home schooling. With home-schooling parents can decide to hire five teachers who can educate their children online. They do not need to send their children to school in that case. If they have to pay one million Kenyan shillings to a school for a whole term and this is a teacher who needs to be paid, let me say 100 or 150,000 Kenyan shillings, that is a lot of savings. If they still learn and they can still do the same exams and they do well, why should I take them to school? So, RTL is here to stay. We will open schools. I am hopeful, maybe next year, these things will have calmed down a little bit. By the end of next year, I am very much hoping that this thing will be over. Of course, life will have changed completely, but remote teaching and learning is here to stay.

Betty Sheila Mumbi

I think so. I do not know why I feel that when someone now calls in sick they have the option of teaching from their house. I just figure cover teaching will be much easier now because we have the option of teaching the kids from our houses. I think the use of technology in learning should continue and I think it will for a lot of students. Obviously, with the exception of students in public schools who have not had the privilege that we have had to keep learning over the past seven months since we closed. I think all international schools have been working online and quite a few Kenyan schools as well. The high-end private schools also have been working online, so it is really just the underprivileged schools that have not been learning; otherwise most schools have been learning online.

Hubert Mweli

Running the bureaucracy had to change from the many face-to-face meetings to virtual meetings. The in-service training for teachers had to follow is all online now. This is now common across the country and this will be a good legacy.

All our business processes are now digitised, and all engagement with stakeholders is online. Another innovation we will try to continue is that we have been able to link up learners with the best teacher for a particular specialism even if they are outside their area.

We have digitised all of our textbooks, which is another good legacy, so our resources are now all digitised. There are 144 Teacher Centres (TCs) around the country, and we can link them all up virtually. We can work with the teachers at the TCs or at their homes.

We have been able to rely on each other, both in government and in education. We are relying more on school-based assessment. Even though we are a country that is driven by public examinations, we have had to use teacher assessment. This has restored confidence in schools and local authorities are now in charge of assessments.

We have learned from each other; we are managing the virus together. I am in education, but I am leading a cluster of cross-disciplinary interests across government to deal with the virus. We are confronting the challenges together, learning from each other, and this has worked well. We must continue to work together in this way. Public schools are working with independent schools; they are sharing resources and ideas. Part of the reason we could cover the curriculum is that schools have shared resources. The government has invested in independent schools so that poorer schools can benefit. We are using the facilities to reach out to the most needy. This helped a lot.

The political parties worked together at first, but along the way this fractured a little as they are competing for voters, but schools are still working together and I hope that will continue. There is serious competition between public and private and competition within the private sector for students. We hope they will continue to work together, although we do rank schools and that might work against schools collaborating in the long run.

Helen Toft

I am sure some of the innovations will stay. Face-to-face inductions for the PGCEi course that I teach on might be gone, partly for financial reasons with the costs of travel and accommodation and so on. I think I have accepted that now. I feel lucky that I have had the opportunity to travel as a part of my educational life. I think being in the same room as people is really important, but it has to make sense environmentally too.

The shared spaces moment with the student in China that I wrote about in a previous chapter has shown me how important making connections with people in their own workspaces has been. During my career I have studied, 'Where and how we learn', researched how to create deep learning spaces and now I see this in a whole new way. There are, of course, ethical issues to be considered if the use of video causes any concerns to learners.

Being able to work simultaneously with different people in different places around the world has impressed me deeply. The image of the faces of five black academics from around the country leading a panel on the impact of the Black Lives Matter (BLM) movement shifted the balance and I hope it was empowering for them. This format should stay; inviting guest lecturers from around the world suddenly feels non-problematic and we would not have thought of this before.

The journey my grandchildren, students and elderly choir members have been on is at once fast and furious and simultaneously slowed down and intense. There are moments when humour, success and deep interest have been stimulated and these moments stay with me in the same way that critical incidents from my classrooms remain vivid memories and influence my teaching to this day.

I am now convinced the connection between participants, teachers and learners can reach just as powerful a level as face to face. Having mentored students in distress to complete their studies effectively, I have experienced the power of this for myself. At a recent choir session Thanda screen shared a 'spoken word' music back tracked by Kate Tempest, 'People's Faces' (2019). This poem moves through a gamut of emotions and deserves several listens, but as a motto for these times the line 'There is so much peace to be found in people's faces' resonated with the people's faces on my computer screen and struck me as a useful example of just how powerful online learning can be.

Delmer Tzib

All of the things that I was doing online I was doing beforehand anyway. One size does not fit all. The new ways of working online are an extension of what I was doing anyway. We are pretty young in the profession and my generation is the generation that is in the transition between moving from the traditional ways to using technology in our day-to-day teaching anyway. For older teachers this whole thing has been a drastic shift.

Louise Whyte

On a day-to-day basis the best innovation for me is the incorporation of more technology in learning. This year students have all been given devices as part of the school development plan and having a record of the students' work stored online avoids some of the issues such as 'I don't have my book'; 'I lost the worksheet'; 'I left that sheet at home'. Some students have shown to be a lot more organised now we are working more online. Using *OneNote*, work can be marked in real time whilst maintaining social distancing, which means that any student who is isolating at home can join the class and have a similar experience to those in school. I think that we have to be mindful that some work should be done on paper; graphs, calculations and written responses can be easily created and edited online, but it takes skill to be able to present this information by hand. External exams remain focused on written exams, even though most workplaces now rely on technology. We need to prepare them for both.

Due to Covid-19 regulations we have gone back to quite a traditional school layout with students remaining in one classroom, sitting in individual desks in rows facing the front. To encourage more dialogue, we are continuing the aim of working more online; students have really got on board with the increase in the use of technology. We can complete work on collaborative platforms and play more online games together in class. If they are doing some homework, they can quickly submit something as simple as a screenshot. We also have a programme that involves artificial intelligence so that students work through a pathway of tasks suited to their level. If they have a question for a teacher, they can send it easily and know that their teacher will respond when they can. Some of the kids who had never asked me a question before or rarely gave an opinion now feel confident enough to communicate with us. Some would always put up their hand or come and find you at break. They still do that, but it is the ones that previously wouldn't accept help in front of others, for a manner of reasons but most often because they are shy or really struggling. They now know that no one else except me will have seen that message. And there are definitely a lot more students who I never would have had that conversation with in the past that I can now. We have all tried so many strategies but they often end up pointing out the student; no 14-year-old wants to put a red card on their desk to indicate they need help, especially if everyone else is green. The other day, a student sent me a message during the lesson and said, 'Can you come and help me when you can?'. They did not want to put their hand up to show that they needed help, but if I made my own way over there then that would be fine. They had a voice.

Vicky Van Wyk

I have learnt a great deal from online classes. In my opinion, I thought it was easier to attract children's attention on the screen than in the classroom. Apart from the inquisitive parents, there were fewer distractions than in the class. For my own well-being, I had to remind myself to take a breather once in a while. As many teachers did, I tried incredibly hard to keep students interested and keen to learn, which meant I used all of my available energy to keep this up, which in turn left very little to myself.

I would like to continue my daily check-ins with the students, making sure they know there is someone listening to them. I think student-centred teaching needs to be a priority in classrooms when schools open back up. I have realised with my own experience that I would easily pick up cues during online learning that something might be amiss with a student, or that they may not be comprehending what is being taught during the lesson. More so than in the classroom unfortunately, which is an aspect of my teaching that needs to be adapted.

I loved being creative and goofy online; it made me connect with many more of my students on different levels. But in school, the atmosphere felt more formal in a sense, restricting the amusement in class. I am aware that students need to learn, and all schools have curriculums they have to abide by, but these students are also very young. At this age, they are meant to have fun, play and not take life too seriously. So, if that means coming to school in a scuba outfit to teach them about the ocean, I am all for it. It would create magical moments for these young ones, where they would more easily remember the lesson if it were interactive and play based, rather than rote learning. Moreover, it would be fun!

Reflections

To some extent we were all on the road to some form of blended learning from the fully blended experience of the participants on the University of Nottingham's to fairly straightforward use of technology in some classrooms. Perhaps the experience of the pandemic has moved us all more quickly down that road than would otherwise have been the case. One image for the future might be that class sizes are reduced or that teacher contact time becomes only a part of the learning experience in school. So, some of a learners time in school would be spent in an individual or group learning space working individually or with a small group on self-study activities. This would be supported by less, but more personalised teacher contact time. Edward and Jess describe in their entries above how important the parents have become in the current blend of home schooling and teacher-led learning. This may well become increasingly important. Jasmine also describes how the use of technology is allowing her team to become more personal in their approach to the support her learners require.

Jess describes how she wants to continue using the platforms she is operating with to give individual and targeted feedback. These platforms also offer learners a range of ways to 'submit' their responses to activities which can quickly be responded to by the teachers. Perhaps formative feedback will become increasingly important, taking precedence over summative feedback. Vicky gives an example of how this may happen through her daily check-ins with her students. Several of these stories do contain a warning for us all. There is a sense that in some schools there is a quick reversion to what went on before. It would be a great shame and a huge waste of all the energy from teachers that has gone into innovation if we simply go back to the old ways of doing things. Perhaps there may be a need for a slight pause, a time to take a breath back in school before we use what we have learned to transform the educational experience of our learners.

Another innovation that could remain is making use of a wider range of spaces for learning. A range of spaces in schools and community and public spaces could become learning centres. All that would be needed would be a bank of computers and access to the internet. In this way learning could be accessed by the whole community, not just the students enrolled in schools. As Mr Muhati suggests, this may make a high-quality education much more affordable in those countries where educating our children can be an expensive business. It may also mean that students can access learning if extreme weather conditions or travel difficulties mean they cannot physically get to the school. It also means that students with chronic illnesses could become full members of the class.

Hubert Mweli offers a wider view. He suggests that political parties and governments need to work together, in partnership on developing education for the good of all of society. It is a time when we must work together rather than pull apart or represent partisan constituencies. The public and private sectors of education must cooperate to make sure all learners in their countries have access to the best resources.

When some of the older members of the writing team were training as teachers it was common to visualise the classroom of the future. This image (recalled from 40 years ago) was of a robot teaching classes of children or every child sitting at a computer terminal. This felt like a dystopic view to many of us as the teacher seemed to be written out of the future of education. Perhaps this book is exploring the ways in which the teacher and learning can harness the potential of technology rather than be replaced by it.

Finally, the issue of the environment may have become side-lined for a while whilst government's energies were focused on fighting the pandemic but we are in a very different place now in regards to travel. We should all think very carefully about how much travel is necessary, and surely, photocopying is a thing of the past.

Which changes in your practice do you think will continue in your classroom-based teaching?

Chapter 11

A global vision for the future

This chapter was written as a collaborative venture by all the contributors to the book. Once all the interviews had been completed and the chapters that you have just read were completed, Lucy, Helen and Tony set up a meeting for all the contributors using *Teams*. This meeting was held on Saturday, 30 January; ironically Vicky and Ed in Bangkok could not attend as they had been called into school at short notice to clean and prepare for the return of the pupils on the following Monday. Delmer in Belize was recovering from his own illness with Covid-19 and connection problems also added a challenge, but all of these issues mirrored the challenges of education in the current times. We were able to catch up with all the contributors at a later date, and we hope that this chapter shows how technology can be used to share thoughts, to envision a future and to write collaboratively.

One of the first books that Tony wrote explored how primary education could impact the whole community. The model he drew on was that of the primary school of which he was chair of governors; his close colleague and friend Jasbir was head, and perhaps most importantly both Tony and Jasbir's children attended. As Jasbir took on the role of headteacher they decided that the whole community should be involved in discussing, implementing and monitoring a mission for the school. Representatives from the local communities and a range of parents all attended a development day. During the day this group worked on three questions:

- What does an educated person look like in the post-pandemic world? What skills, attributes and attitudes do they have?
- What sorts of teachers will these educated people have had guiding them? What skills, attributes and attitudes will these teachers have had?
- What educational experiences are all learners entitled to in order to become 'educated'?

DOI: 10.4324/9781003150596-11

We thought that these three questions would serve this group of writers well as we tried to offer a mission for education at a global level, post-pandemic. The first point we could agree on quickly was that education should not return to the practices pre-pandemic. We must learn from our experiences.

So, the first question:

What skills, attributes and attitudes does an educated person have in the post-pandemic world?

As we reflected on this question we wondered if the pandemic had made it harder to be or become an 'educated person'. We wondered if learners' ability to focus was declining or is becoming lost through a lack of access to classrooms. We realised that many students are being asked to operate in an adult way in that there is an expectation of individual responsibility for learning and engagement. We wondered how remote learning might support resilience which was something we saw as important. It is hard to support the development of resilience remotely.

Some colleagues suggested that it had become harder to share challenging activities with learners. And challenge is a key part of learning. If we are not being challenged in our learning, we are just repeating things we already know. We are doing stuff, but we are not learning stuff! But what do we do if our learners respond by saying, 'This work is too hard I can't even do it'. It has become harder during the second lockdown which occurred, at different times around the world, for teachers to control and develop online learning. Schools and governments seem to have been more prescriptive in terms of curriculum coverage and the ways in which this curriculum should be experienced by learners.

But we also saw evidence of learners taking control. For example, when presented with asynchronous learning resources they may stop an introductory exposition when they think they have understood enough to proceed and fast forward to the activity itself, returning to the exposition if they hit a difficulty. This perhaps mirrors the way that people read online materials such as magazines or blogs. They read and interact with online materials in a very different way from print media. They do not start at the beginning and read through to the end. They select pieces, skip over others and return to those articles they are interested in.

We also have some evidence that through the shared experience, which is living and learning under the pandemic, we have started to share our humanity. We share the same worries as our learners, and we have realised that we can care for each other as we live through a crisis none of us has experienced before.

Before you read on we invite you to reflect for yourself on this question. Perhaps one way to explore the question is to think of someone, or several people, who you regard as 'well-educated'.

What skills, attributes and attitudes does an educated person have?

We saw an educated person as someone who is continually curious. A genuine lifelong learner who notices things in their environment; reads about things in the media; experiences things with friends and colleagues and wants to be able to find out more about them. Perhaps more importantly they have developed the skills to research or will take the opportunity to develop new research skills through finding out more. Educated people 'revel in their ignorance'. They see not knowing about something as an opportunity to learn rather than a personal lack of ignorance. The discovery of an area of ignorance is an opportunity to broaden our experience. Educated people do not see knowledge as simply being able to regurgitate facts; they understand that it is much broader than that. In fact, they do not measure themselves or others through success in external examinations. They see education as giving them the responsibility to act for the good of the community.

They are adaptable and flexible. They are able to change to meet challenges that they were not expecting and are patient when they are not immediately successful or when they don't immediately succeed at whatever they are engaging in. This can also be seen in their resilience, their discipline and perseverance. We see educated people sticking to a task.

An educated person will take creative inspiration from their lived experiences. They may share or reflect on these experiences by writing poetry; creating art; or inventing and playing games. This creativity allows them to feel at ease in the world. Educated people share learning. They see learning as a communal activity and something that everyone can do and can do together. They are able to make other people feel at ease in the world by modelling how to live creatively. This 'ease with the world' can be seen in their ability to have fun and to share this 'fun' with family, friends and colleagues. Educated people are committed to this sharing of learning.

Educated people work at using new technologies to exploit possibilities for learning and for sharing learning. They are able to question data and do not take stories from the media at face value. They read and observe critically and only act when they have a full understanding of particular situations.

Educated people are empathetic. They act as support for others and do not seek to exert power or dominate others. They act and operate at a global level and understand the concept of the world as a global village. They are also compassionate. They understand what it is that makes us human and what connects us. They are not afraid of exposing their vulnerability and accept that sometimes it is vulnerability that brings us together. In fact, the pandemic is a perfect example of that.

Finally, educated people take their own and others' well-being seriously.

To summarise. Students who have become educated:

- Are curious
- Are adaptable and flexible
- Are at ease in the world
- Draw on their life experiences creatively
- Interpret data and ideas critically
- Use new technologies effectively
- Are empathetic in their relationships with others
- Act compassionately
- Use their learning for the benefit of their communities
- Look after their well-being

> Think about the lessons you taught last week. Which of the aptitudes above did your teaching support the development of?

What sorts of teachers will these educated people have had guiding them?

Of course, the simple and obvious answer is that teachers should be educated people themselves. They should have all the attributes and qualities that have been described above. But, there is more to it than that. Not every educated person would make a great teacher and not every educated person would want to be a teacher. We tried to unpick the question a little bit more. What would it be that set these teachers, educating learners across the global, apart from what has come before?

What skills, attributes and attitudes will teachers need to support their learners in developing into educated people?

We suggested that an educated person would see learning as a collaborative experience and be a curious lifelong learner. So, the first thing we would hope to see in a teacher is that they themselves are a learner who shares the experience of learning with their students. They will be passionate about learning and will be able to draw on this passion to develop and encourage curiosity in the students they teach. They will feed the imaginations of their students and support them in becoming good questioners. In fact, in this teacher's classroom we would hear lots of questions and very few answers.

This teacher will be able to tailor the curriculum and the learning experience to individuals. Like all good coaches they will have high expectations and will know when students need support, when they need challenge, when they need rewards, when they need more firm encouragement. They will know what captures individual's interests and will seek this out. They understand how important it is to let, and expect, students to ask questions about issues that are interesting them at the moment. They understand that the curriculum has to be stretched to allow students to explore these interests. They are flexible enough in their approach to know how and when they can deviate from an imposed curriculum.

They will be compassionate too. They understand that everyone has challenges and that some learners have to overcome huge challenges. They will be non-judgemental and be able to 'capture' those who are having a difficult time learning. You know that teacher who seems to attract all the kids with difficulties to their room at lunchtime? They are the sort of teacher we are talking about.

This teacher does not just enthuse people to learn, but students are motivated to learn because of the model that the teacher provides. They understand that people think and learn in different ways. They will encourage those who like to learn on their own to share their ideas with others when it is appropriate, and they will find ways of developing individual research skills for those who would rather always work as a part of a group. In fact, these teachers revel in diversity. They want a classroom, virtual or otherwise, to contain learners with a wide range of experience; students who can speak many languages; students whose brains and bodies work in different ways. These teachers will find ways to bring the whole world into their classroom, perhaps something we are learning to do more effectively as we discover new tools for learning and teaching.

These teachers will show and model empathy. In their relationships with colleagues and with students they will model how to support each other rather than tearing each other down. They will show how it is possible to have power with colleagues and students as opposed to exerting power over others. We wondered if we have got better at this through the pandemic. Perhaps we have become closer with our learners through our shared experience of the pandemic. For many of us working with our students was the highlight of our week. We all heard stories of teachers taking food to the families they knew who were struggling to feed their children and who were raising money to provide students with the technology they needed to access learning. These are the good teachers.

These teachers are at ease with technology or at least happy to try things and learn. They will take risks with new technologies to discover what is possible. These will be the people that are helping to create the tools that we need rather than just relying on other people to provide platforms.

Great teachers have great global networks that they can draw on to support and inspire learners and to develop themselves as teachers and as human beings. They will also spend time and energy building networks so that everyone can benefit from a wide range of teachers with a wide range of skills.

These teachers will have a broad range of skills and abilities but may also have a particular area of specialism which they will enjoy sharing with their students and the students will love being exposed to this passion. Finally, good teachers take their well-being seriously. They look after themselves. They understand we need to look after our own well-being; we need to be physically and mentally well, in order to support our students and look after their own well-being.

Reflections

Perhaps, as with our previous book *Being a teacher*, these reflections are best set out as a series of competencies. For those of us engaged in teacher education we can reflect on how we might design a teacher education course to support the development of these competencies.

A successful teacher will be:

A lifelong learner. They will share this learning with the students they teach and with colleagues. Their enthusiasm about the new things they are learning will be infectious.

A collaborator and a networker. They will have a wide range of contacts that they can draw upon to support their teaching. Students will see their teacher collaborating through team teaching both physically and online.

An innovator. They will be well read and up-to-date about the latest research and developments in educational thinking and will draw on these to innovate in their own practice.

Someone who can motivate their students. They will be able to offer both extrinsic motivation and support intrinsic motivation. They will motivate through example and through expertise.

Empathetic. They will understand the individual situations of their students and know when to encourage and when to support as well as what kind of encouragement and support is necessary.

Technologically literate. Through collaboration and research they will understand the opportunities offered by the latest technological developments. They will use these to innovate in their classrooms.

A specialist in one or more areas. They will share this specialism with their students, who will revel in their teacher's abilities and draw on their teacher's enthusiasm for this area.

Concerned about their well-being. They will look after themselves and in this way offer a positive role model to their students.

Which of the above skills do you think you have? How do you know?

Which of the above skills would you like to develop next?

Chapter 12

Entitlements for all learners

Throughout all our conversations we were reminded of the inequities present in education. The narrative from Hubert Mweli describing the situation at a national level makes it clear that in South Africa the government was particularly aware of the difficulties that many children were having in accessing online learning. Similarly, Amanda and Delmer describe their frustrations as they realise that many of their learners are struggling to access their teaching due to a lack of equipment or poor access to the internet. There has always been unequal access to educational opportunities. We wonder if this has been exacerbated by the pandemic. Education only became possible at all if the learner had access to technology. Many schools expected learners to be able to access the internet. For many learners this was not possible. Whereas unequal access previously has been through lack of access to a physical school, now unequal access includes not having access to appropriate technology.

The other side of the coin is that where this problem is being solved some learners can gain more access to teaching. Tony received an email this morning asking him to support children in refugee camps through online mathematics lessons – something that would not be possible if only face-to-face teaching was possible.

UNICEF reported (www.unicef.org/press-releases/unequal-access-remote-schooling-amid-covid-19-threatens-deepen-global-learning) that despite less than half the population having access to the internet in 71 countries, 73% of governments are using online platforms for teaching and learning whilst schools are closed. Television has also been widely used; 75% of countries reported using national television channels to support learning. This brings its own disparities. For example, in rural Chad only 1% of households have a television compared to 75% of

DOI: 10.4324/9781003150596-12

homes in urban areas. Radio is the third most used platform for remote learning, with 60% of countries reporting using the radio. This has been particularly popular in Latin America and the Caribbean.

Surely, as a global society, we should be able to create such opportunities. Perhaps a small proportion of the budgets allocated in the rich world to fight the virus could be allocated to support all learners in gaining access to a virtual classroom.

The same UNICEF report goes on to detail successes in transforming access to remote learning, including:

> Governments in West and Central Africa are working with local service providers to support distance learning for primary and lower secondary age children online or through radio, TV, and paper-based approaches.

In Timor-Leste, the distance learning programme *Eskola ba Uma* or *School Goes Home* is using television, radio and other online platforms to allow children to continue learning. For those without access to any of these options, UNICEF partnered with Telenor, a mobile phone provider, to give 600,000 mobile phone users in rural areas free access to learning materials.

In Somalia, offline recorded lessons are being uploaded onto solar-powered tablets and made available to children. Video lessons are also shared through social media channels such as *WhatsApp* and *Facebook* and broadcast through radio and TV. In Mongolia, TV has been the main medium for distance learning. UNICEF has worked with the Mongolian government to produce TV lessons for pre-primary and primary education in Tuvan and Kazakh languages to reach children from ethnic minorities. They have also partnered with the local government to produce offline learning materials to support the learning of primary school children in remote areas who have limited access to TV and/or the internet.

In Kyrgyzstan, children can access remote learning through online platforms, three national TV channels and two mobile network applications free of charge. UNICEF also supported the development and dissemination of content for children with special education needs by ensuring all remote learning lessons are also provided through sign language. Subtitles for all lessons are also provided in Uzbek and Tajik minority languages to ensure no child is left behind. Similarly, in Jamaica, the Ministry of Education is providing lessons at all levels through national public television, radio, online platforms, and *WhatsApp*. Work is also underway to organise access for 210 of the most vulnerable students to tablets equipped with connectivity and content to facilitate ongoing schooling.

These are all examples of how UNICEF and the national government can work together to ensure that learners have access to the physical resources they need to be able to access education. If one of the results of the way in which education is transformed as a result of the pandemic is that more children have access to these physical resources, that will be a great step forward. It may even move us, as a global society of educators, towards the second millennium goal of the achievement of universal primary education. But, and there is a big but, education is about much more than simply having access to the tools. What sort of curriculum is fit for all the learners in the 21st century? This is the big question that we have been tackling as we explore our teaching over the last year or so. We have had to adapt our teaching quickly; we have had to get used to new ways of teaching; we have observed what has been successful and what has been less successful. So, what have we learned?

A curriculum for the 21st century

One way to offer an image of such a curriculum is to take an imaginary walk through an educational setting that is offering such a curriculum. You can then take a walk through your own setting and use the bulleted list at the end of this section to review the current educational experience of your learners.

As we enter the school we are welcomed by learners. They have the responsibility of welcoming visitors and making sure they find their way to the correct place. The learners are confident, are expecting us and talk animatedly about the setting and the other visitors they are expecting during the day. The displays in the entrance hall show that the setting is well networked globally – there is a world map showing all the connections. These are connections that the learners and teachers have, as well as other places which the setting is working with. There is also a display entitled 'Issue of the week' – this uses extracts from local and national media and poses a question which all the different groups in the school will work on for the week. The children that have welcomed us say that there is a whole school meeting using the school's learning platform at the end of the week where they will all report back on their responses.

We can see into the school hall as we pass by and there is a school meeting being led by one of the members of the school council. They have been asked by the school management team to audit the setting's impact on the environment. They are holding a 'town-hall meeting' with representatives from all ages of learners to write an action plan for the setting. We notice that there is a panel of experts from around the world appearing using the school's online learning platform.

There are several open spaces on the way to the classroom, all occupied by learners using the computer terminals to access online activities. They work in pairs and threes on these activities. They talk animatedly about what they are exploring and are enjoying preparing newspaper reports; short videos; presentations; poems and other creative responses, which they will take back to what they call their 'base-room' later in the day.

We move into the classroom and the first thing that we notice is laughter; the learners are working in groups in different sorts of places. There is an animated chatter, but much laughter. The learners clearly enjoy being in the setting. There are many displays, both on the walls and hanging from the roof. Many of these take the forms of questions. The teachers are not immediately visible, but then we see them sitting on the floor with a group of learners. They are listening carefully to the learners as they explain what they have found out as a result of research. Another group is listening carefully to another adult, an expert from the local community who has come into the classroom to share their skills.

As we leave the classroom, we pass several smaller interview rooms. In one of these rooms a teacher sits with a learner and their parents. The learner is leading the conversation and we overhear them sharing their successes and setting future learning targets with both the teachers and their parent. The parent and teacher are discussing the ways in which they can best support the learner in meeting their learning targets.

To summarise – we invite you to use this list to audit the current curriculum you offer your learners in your setting. We would aim to offer learners in our settings:

- A seriously playful curriculum
- A joyful curriculum
- A questioning and critical curriculum (not giving answers)

- A curriculum that gives learners voice, choice and control
- A curriculum that expects communication
- A contemporary curriculum – deals with questions that are facing learners at the moment
- A curriculum that celebrates diversity in all its forms
- A curriculum that supports and develops diverse learning and thinking styles
- A curriculum that is assessed authentically

The last words belong to you:

Index

Andreotti, V. 23, 30
assessment xi, 5, 6, 25, 36, 70, 102, 124, 126, 154, 157
asynchronous learning 65, 168
Australia xv, 4, 5, 7–8, 24, 34, 35, 123
Autism Spectrum Condition (ASC) 36, 93

Bangkok xiv, xvi, xviii, 32, 34, 42, 43, 53, 76, 90, 143, 167
beliefs 20, 22, 43, 146
Belize xv, xvii, 7–8, 32, 41, 53, 66, 70, 90, 116, 121, 130, 137, 167
Black Lives Matter (BLM) 82, 141, 159
blended learning xiii, 153, 162
Boaler, J. 124
Bobek, E. 10
Bottery, M. 20, 30
Brazil, xii, xvii, 7–8, 44, 60, 140
Brighton 36, 138
British Columbia 14, 30

Cambridge Assessment (CAIE) 6
Canada 145
caring 3, 22, 32, 40, 64, 70, 90, 102, 116, 121, 136, 145
cell phones 42, 59
chat function (use of) 60, 91, 101, 102, 145
collaboration xvi, 26, 36, 42, 85, 176
commonplace book xix, 9, 11, 16, 42
communication (effective) 42, 54, 57, 61, 77, 114
communication (problems with) 96, 98, 153
communication (skills) 26, 36, 56, 80
communication (virtual) 13, 63, 85, 91, 114
community (choir) 41, 45, 83
compassion 112, 171, 174

Cooker, L. xx, 32, 51, 75, 105, 119, 135, 151
Cotton, T. xx, 32, 52, 77, 90, 105, 120, 136, 152
covid-19 93, 99
covid-19 (international responses) 7–8
covid-19 (myths) 6–7
creativity xv, xvii, 19, 26, 170
critical thinking xv, 26, 143
cross-curricular teaching xvi, 62, 98
Cuisenaire rods 121

democratic approaches to learning and teaching xx, 14, 30, 130
digital literacy 26, 141
digital resources 139–141
diversity 14, 45, 183
drama xvi, 60

early years xiii, 33–34, 42, 114, 153
Emmett, E. xvi, 33, 44, 53, 78, 92, 106, 121, 137, 146, 153, 162
emotion xvi, 26, 43, 56, 57, 65, 80, 141, 151
empowerment 19
Ernest, P. 17, 20, 22, 30
examination(s) 5, 6, 26, 32, 36, 40, 157, 170

Facebook 180
face-to-face teaching xiii, xiv, 5, 6, 36, 56, 64, 71, 86, 90, 91, 93, 101, 102, 107, 119–120, 138, 141, 152, 154–158, 179
Fasheh, M. 25

global education xiii, 30
global skills xiii, 26–28
google classroom 61, 65, 78, 79, 123, 138, 154

Index

Greenbaum, J. xiv, xv, 34–35, 44–45, 54–55, 70, 92, 102, 107, 116, 122, 137, 145, 154, 162

history (teaching) xvii, 41
Hitler's daughter (novel) 123
hooks, b. xi, xx–xxi
Horne, A (Taskmaster) 107
humanities (teaching) xvii, 39, 63

identity 21, 51, 86, 107
inclusion 69, 102, 124, 151
information technology 18, 34
interaction (in learning) 69, 80
interaction (social) 21, 55, 155
interaction (with colleagues) 84, 128
interaction (with parents) 111, 115
interaction (with students) 96–97
International baccalaureate (IB) 5–6, 153
International rescue committee (IRC) 4, 12
international schools xvii, 26, 38, 43, 115, 120, 138, 157
investigative approaches 125, 131
Irani, J. xvi, 36, 55, 93, 107, 123, 138, 154
isolation 6, 135

Jefferies, S. xvi, 37, 57, 79, 93, 108, 123, 138, 155
Johnston, S. xvii, xviii

Kenya xvii, 7–8, 39, 81, 125
kindergarten xiii, 37, 69, 153

Latham, M. xix
leadership 126, 130, 135
League of Nations 125–126
Lego 123, 138

Mario do Souza, L. 23, 30
mental health 6, 71, 81, 96, 101, 102
mentor 39, 110, 113
millennium goals 4, 181
Minas, M. xiv, 34, 58, 80, 109, 124
Mongolia xvi, 7–8, 37–38, 53, 57, 71, 94, 139, 180
Montessori 33–34
motivation 36, 83, 126, 176
Moura, A. xvii, 38, 58, 80, 95, 108, 124, 139, 156
Muhati, N. xvii, 38, 45, 60, 81, 86, 96, 102, 110, 125, 130, 139, 146, 156, 163

Mumbi, B. xvii, 39, 61, 81, 97, 111, 126, 140, 157
music (activities) 37, 54, 153
music (performance) 40, 53, 98, 159
Mweli, H. xvii, 39, 45, 64, 82, 86, 98, 112, 115, 127, 140, 157, 163, 179
Myanmar xviii, 7–8, 42–43, 68

Nairobi xvii, 38, 39, 61

observation (peer) 138
Onenote 160
online platforms 59, 66, 83, 89, 101, 135, 154, 155, 180–181

PE (teaching) 39, 62, 70
pedagogy 30
pedagogy (student-centred) xv, 19–20, 126
planning (collaboration) 35, 78–80, 86, 138
planning (lesson) 55, 66, 70, 109, 119, 127, 131
playfulness 56, 91, 123, 182
play therapy 42–43, 45

racism xxi, 82
refugees 4, 179
resilience 65, 102, 168, 170
risk (of infection) 5, 82, 108, 154
risk (taking) 146, 175

Sao Paulo xvii, 38, 60, 96
scavenger hunts 123, 129, 131
science (teaching) xviii, 34, 41, 129
social distancing 64, 68, 81, 84, 110, 153–155, 160
South Africa xvii, 7–8, 40–41, 82, 137, 142, 143, 179
Spain xvii, 7–8, 15, 41–42, 142
sports 62, 94, 108, 111

teacher education 32, 70, 175
teaching assistant xiii, 33, 54, 71, 92
Teams (platform) 63, 76, 86, 98, 114, 152, 167
Tempest, K. 159
Thailand xvi, 7–8, 33, 53–54, 112, 142, 153
Toft, H. xx, 40, 82, 98, 112, 127, 141, 158
trauma 43, 82
Tversky, B. 10
Tzib, D. xvii, 41, 65, 83, 99, 113, 127, 160

UNESCO 3, 27
UNICEF 12, 14, 22, 179–181
University of Nottingham xv, xvi, 32, 40, 45

Van Wyk, V. xvii, 3, 42, 68, 85, 101, 115, 129, 161
video (use of online) 52, 55, 138
video (for teaching) 57, 63, 66, 76, 79, 123, 139, 153, 154, 180

Walton, E. xvii, xviii
Webinars 32, 33, 70, 91, 120, 136

well-being 15, 43, 175
WhatsApp 60, 84, 86, 105, 106, 137, 152, 180, 181
Whyte, L. xviii, 41, 67, 84, 100, 114, 128, 143, 160
World Health Organisation (WHO) 6, 12

YouTube xii, 35, 44, 59, 71, 122, 127

Zoom 55–57, 61, 69, 79, 85, 91, 93, 123, 138, 146, 152, 154
Zoom (and parents) 107, 108, 155
Zoom (choir) 83, 98, 99

For Product Safety Concerns and Information please contact our EU representative GPSR@taylorandfrancis.com
Taylor & Francis Verlag GmbH, Kaufingerstraße 24, 80331 München, Germany

www.ingramcontent.com/pod-product-compliance
Lightning Source LLC
Chambersburg PA
CBHW071957240426
43669CB00049B/2682